GEOFFREY N. WRIGHT

Discovering
Abbeys and Priories

A SHIRE BOOK

Published in 2010 by Shire Publications Ltd, Midland House, West Way, Botley, Oxford
OX2 0PH, UK. (Website: www.shirebooks.co.uk)

British Library Cataloguing in Publication Data: Wright, Geoffrey N. (Geoffrey
Norman), Discovering Abbeys and Priories. – 4th ed. – (Discovering; 57) 1. Monastic
and religious life – History 2. Monasteries – Great Britain – History 3. Monasteries –
Great Britain – Guidebooks 4. Great Britain – Church history I. Title 255'.00941'0902.
ISBN-10: 0 7478 0589 X.

ACKNOWLEDGEMENTS
  Photographs are acknowledged as follows: Chertsey Museum, page 93; David Ross,
pages 1, 126; Geoffrey N. Wright, pages 26, 28, 31, 35 (top), 86. All other photographs,
including the front cover, are by Cadbury Lamb.

Front cover: *Fountains Abbey, Yorkshire.*
Title page: *Dorchester Abbey, Oxfordshire.*

Printed in China through Worldprint Ltd.

Kirkham Priory, Yorkshire: the fourteenth-century gatehouse.

Contents

✤ ✤ ✤ ✤ ✤ ✤

Titchfield Abbey, Hampshire: the turreted gatehouse.

Tewkesbury Abbey, Gloucestershire: bought by the town after the Dissolution for use as a parish church.

Introduction

✢ ✢ ✢ ✢ ✢ ✢

The word 'abbey' may conjure up different things to different people. To some it may mean the idea of a splendid church, as at Bath, Malmesbury, Selby, Sherborne, Romsey or Westminster; to others it may bring a vision of an exquisite ruin in very picturesque surroundings, as at Rievaulx, Tintern or Dryburgh; others may even associate the word with an elegant country mansion, as at Lacock, Wiltshire, and Newstead, Nottinghamshire. In addition, many famous cathedrals are referred to as 'cathedral-priories' and some famous ruins are priories – a name also used for some parish churches and, with less justification, for country houses.

All this is rather confusing. The aim of this book is to clarify matters. It seeks to explain how Britain's monasteries came into being, the importance of their churches and the significance of the various domestic buildings associated with them, and tells of the monks whose lives were spent there up to the Dissolution of the Monasteries in the first half of the sixteenth century.

Over seventy of Britain's monastic ruins are in official guardianship, either of English Heritage, Historic Scotland or Cadw (for those in Wales), and are therefore readily accessible to the public, either freely or at an admission charge. A few, including the important ones of Buckland Abbey, Fountains Abbey and Lacock Abbey, are in the care of the National Trust and, like others under private ownership such as Beaulieu, Forde and Glastonbury, are open at certain times. Many monastic churches or parts of churches are now in parochial use and can readily be seen, as can the cathedral-priories and Westminster Abbey. For some of these an entrance fee is now charged. A gazetteer of the more important monastic remains is given at the end of the book, with descriptions of the things to be seen at each.

Criteria for inclusion of an abbey or ruin are that the visible ruins are of monastic or architectural importance, or both; they can be visited on site, or be seen from a nearby road or public footpath, and have sufficient of interest to justify either a special visit or a short detour on a journey. Monastic churches now in parochial or cathedral use are included usually for their architectural quality, sometimes for their surviving claustral buildings.

Since the first edition of this book was published there has been an increasing amount of interest in monastic archaeology. Major excavations have taken place at Norton Priory and at various earthwork sites such as Bordesley and Thornholme. Fountains Abbey has become the most intensively studied of all Cistercian houses. It should be borne in mind while walking round the ruins of monasteries that the buildings now seen are only the last of those on a site which had been occupied for up to four hundred years, during which time many changes will have taken place to accommodate new ideas, economic fluctuations, developments in monastic life and changes in liturgy. It should also be remembered that monasteries were important economic corporations whose activities affected the whole of medieval England, as well as much of Wales and Scotland.

The Saxon church at Bradford-on-Avon, Wiltshire.

The earliest monasteries

✣ ✣ ✣ ✣ ✣ ✣

Since the very earliest days of Christianity there have been men who preferred to leave the everyday life of the world in order to devote their lives to prayer and the worship of God. These first monks – the word 'monk' means 'solitary' – lived alone as hermits in lonely caves or in crude cells. When, in time, monks banded together into small communities, monasteries developed.

Christianity first reached Britain during Roman times, and the first British Christian martyr was Alban, a Roman citizen, after whom the Hertfordshire town of St Albans is named. In the fifth century, when heathen invaders from the continent had overrun the lowlands, the Roman Celts who had fled westwards to the lonely hills of Cornwall, Wales and Strathclyde gained strength from their old Christian faith. They built simple wooden chapels and established tiny monasteries with enclosed grass lawns, or 'llans', and these places are marked on maps today with the prefixes of 'capel' and 'llan'.

St Patrick carried this Christian faith to Ireland in the fifth century, and his Irish monks lived in separate tiny cells of earth or stone with thatched roofs but probably met together for church services and meals. From Ireland, St Columba carried the faith to Scotland, where he founded a monastery at Iona, also a collection of separate cells. From there, the Christian faith spread to the north of England, carried by Columba's monks, who, throughout Northumbria, preached, healed and won the hearts of men. In 597, the year that Columba died, St Augustine brought Christianity back to the south of England and established England's first Benedictine monastery at Canterbury, a very different one from those in the far west and in Northumbria.

THE BENEDICTINE RULES

St Benedict was an Italian monk who had initially lived in a cave as a hermit but later realised that monks living in a community could serve God more fully than as solitary individuals. In the year 529 he founded the first of his fourteen Italian monasteries, at Monte Cassino, near Naples. In its community his monks lived a life of prayer, hard work, self-discipline and good deeds, following a set of rules which Benedict had written out in his own hand. These demanded from the monks vows of poverty, obedience and chastity, and they also provided a timetable for the monk's day. This was divided into three parts: first, the work of God, carried out by the eight daily services in church; second, the work in the cloisters – meditation, writing, translating, copying manuscripts and illuminating them; third, work in the fields and gardens to provide necessary food and clothing, or in the form of craftsmanship in sculpture, carving or metalwork.

THE ANGLO-SAXON MONASTERIES

St Augustine's foundation of the great monastery of St Peter and St Paul at Canterbury started a continuous history of almost a thousand years of Benedictine rule in Britain. From Canterbury the Roman monks took their missions westwards to Wessex, where Glastonbury became the most famous monastery. In the north, Columba's monks had spread their influence, and later disciples of Aidan moved southwards into the Midlands – Mercia, as it was called. By the seventh century England had become a Christian country, and in the next century national genius began to flower in the earliest churches at Brixworth in Northamptonshire, Escomb in Durham and Bradford-on-Avon in Wiltshire, as well as in the beautifully sculptured Celtic crosses at Bewcastle in Cumbria, and Ruthwell, in Dumfries and Galloway, carved by Northumbrian monks.

These Anglo-Saxon monasteries were famous throughout Europe as centres of learning and the arts. The first English books were copied and decorated by monks in their tiny cells, the most superb of all being the achievements of the Venerable Bede, the greatest eighth-century scholar in all Europe. In his little monastery cell at Jarrow he wrote a stream of books, on poetry, theology, history, grammar and science, and the most famous of all his works was his *Ecclesiastical History of the English Nation* – clear, just and learned. Bede introduced to England the idea of dating years from the birth of Christ, and he left to his countrymen the earliest translation of the Gospel of St John into their own language, the last sentences of which he dictated as he lay dying on the floor of his monastery cell. Bede is now buried in Durham Cathedral, the great monastic building dedicated to another north-country monk, St Cuthbert, who had become Bishop of Lindisfarne, where the exquisitely lovely Lindisfarne Gospel had been produced. This remarkable work is now in the British Museum. The monastic church in which Bede worshipped survives as the sanctuary of St Paul's church, Jarrow.

Two centuries of Danish invasions, from the eighth century to the tenth, brought regular monastic life to an end, and it was not until the second half of the tenth century that its revival became possible. The monasteries of Northumbria and the Fen Country had by then been destroyed, and only those at Canterbury and in the Celtic west had survived.

A Wessex monk, Dunstan, became Abbot of Glastonbury, where he soon made his monastery famous throughout England for its music, its teaching and its services. In 960 he was made Archbishop of Canterbury and, with his great reformers Ethelwold, Bishop of Winchester, and Oswald, Bishop of York, he was largely responsible for reviving Benedictine rule in its original form, at Bath, Worcester, Cerne, Abingdon, Winchcombe, Eynsham, Crowland, Peterborough, Ely and Bury St Edmunds, as well as Winchester and Glastonbury itself. By the time of the Norman Conquest there were thirty-five monasteries and nine nunneries, all Benedictine.

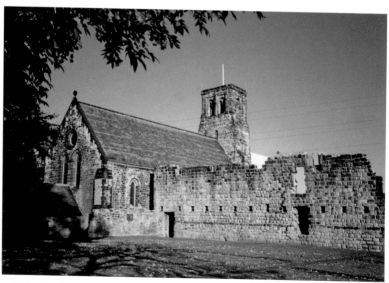

St Paul's church, Jarrow, County Durham, and the remains of a later monastery.

The monastic orders

✣ ✣ ✣ ✣ ✣ ✣

THE BENEDICTINES

Until the time of the Norman Conquest the only monasteries in the western church, apart from a few surviving Celtic ones, followed the Benedictine rule. England's new king, William I, came from Normandy, where Benedictinism flourished more than anywhere else in western Europe, except England, so it was almost inevitable that English Benedictine houses would gain from the Conquest.

William founded Battle Abbey in 1067. By 1100 many more had followed, with Benedictines being installed into a number of cathedrals: Canterbury, Chester, Durham, Ely, Gloucester, Norwich, Peterborough, Rochester, St Albans, Winchester and Worcester, as well as at Bury St Edmunds, Pershore, Romsey and Tewkesbury. By 1215 the number of Benedictine houses had increased to about 225, the vast majority being small or very small, with only a handful of any size. With few exceptions, Benedictine nunneries were poor.

Benedictine monks accumulated books and manuscripts in their libraries. They studied, copied, illustrated and bound books. The scriptorium was often the busiest part of a house. Some monks were artists, some craftsmen, some gardeners, some physicians. From the Benedictines came monastic and national chronicles, and works of scholarship and art.

But towards the end of the eleventh century, and in the twelfth, monasticism grew very rapidly, hundreds of new monasteries were built, and several new monastic orders were founded. Most of these arose from the fact that many existing Benedictine monasteries had become both worldly and wealthy, and the new orders represented a return to the simpler and stricter rules of monastic life which St Benedict had originally laid down.

Thus the new orders, differing only in their interpretations of the rule, were called after the monastic houses which had made the various breakaways. Most of these were in France, and from those at Citeaux and Cluny were derived the anglicised Cistercian and Cluniac orders.

THE CISTERCIANS

Citeaux Abbey had been founded at the end of the eleventh century, and its set of rules was drawn up by an English abbot, Stephen Harding of Dorset, with Bernard, a young French nobleman. The Cistercian order was a strict one, and its rule did not allow its monks to build monasteries in towns. Instead, wild places far away from worldly affairs had to be chosen. The first Cistercian foundation in England was at Waverley, 2 miles (3 km) south-east of Farnham in Surrey, established in 1128. Practically nothing of it remains above ground. The main expansion of the Cistercian order took place in the north of England and in Wales, where few Benedictine monasteries existed, and where vast areas of wild and uncultivated land gave the Cistercian monks the necessary opportunities for their pioneering endeavours.

Unlike the Benedictines, the Cistercians insisted on hard manual work and accepted no gifts other than land. Thus they became great farmers, and on the northern and Welsh hills they kept thousands of sheep, whose wool was subsequently sold to pay for the erection of their monastic churches. Their rule initially forbade them use of any ornament or decoration in their churches, but this was later relaxed. They were allowed to wear only robes of coarse white cloth, and the wearing of this habit resulted in their being called the White Monks, as opposed to the Black Monks, which was the name given to the Benedictines and later to the Cluniacs.

A Benedictine monk (left) and a Cistercian monk (right).

Cistercian monks lived lives of hard work, silence and prayer, and, being of necessity self-supporting, they developed great skills, not only in farming and shepherding, but also in the construction of mills and watercourses for the use of the monastery. They mined metal ores from the Yorkshire hills, they established local industries, and they even owned boats with which overseas trade was carried out.

The Cistercian order did not allow the employment of servants but, as it did attract quite large numbers of uneducated men from rural districts, the monks were divided into two classes: the choir monks, who attended all church services and looked after the running of the monastery; and the lay brothers, who did most of the heavy labour and the farmwork. Because the Cistercians acquired vast estates, particularly on the Pennines and the Yorkshire Moors, some of the farmlands were too distant to be worked from the monastery, so outlying cells called granges, with barns and stables, were built and these were looked after by the lay brothers. For example, much of Borrowdale, in the Lake District, belonged to Furness Abbey, some 30 miles (50 km) away, and the village of Grange-in-Borrowdale got its name from the fact that a monastic grange of the abbey had been established there by the thirteenth century.

Between 1128 and 1152, when the first period of Cistercian settlement had come to an end, about fifty Cistercian monasteries had been founded. Of each of them it could reasonably be said that the monks had taken over a wilderness and turned it into a garden or, more accurately, into a sheep run. This was certainly the case over much of northern England, where wool production on the Cistercian estates led to a medieval export trade which made an enormous contribution to England's prosperity throughout the Middle Ages. The Cistercians shared in this prosperity, so that they too became rich without wanting to, and much of their original zeal and strictness gradually vanished. Beautiful towers were added to their churches, exemplified at Fountains Abbey by Abbot Huby's tower of about 1500.

Large Cistercian foundations such as Fountains or Rievaulx might have accommodated as many as 150 choir monks and 500 lay brothers at the height of their prosperity in the thirteenth century. Of the seventy-five Cistercian abbeys and twenty-six nunneries which were eventually established, few were as enormous as this, but nevertheless these numbers do give some indication of the vastness and importance to the community of Cistercian foundations in remote places. Perhaps it is the rural setting of Cistercian abbeys that gives their ruins the ability to capture the imagination of the thousands who visit such sites as Fountains, Rievaulx and Tintern.

THE CLUNIACS

Although the Cluniac order had been founded as long ago as 910, at Cluny in France, its influence did not spread until the Norman Conquest. Monks of this order wore a black habit, like the Benedictines, and devoted much of their time to church services, leaving the work in the gardens and fields to paid servants. Lewes was the first Cluniac foundation in England, and by 1160 there were thirty-six Cluniac houses, mostly very small cells housing only four or five monks. Castle Acre, Thetford and Wenlock are good surviving examples of larger Cluniac foundations.

THE CARTHUSIANS

The Carthusian order takes its name from the French town of Chartreuse, where the first Carthusian monastery was founded by St Bruno in the twelfth century. It represented a breakaway from the Cluniacs and aimed at a yet more simple and severe life of purity and piety. Carthusian monks lived in almost complete solitude and complete silence, rather in the manner of the early hermits, yet still belonging to a community. Each monk had his little cottage-like cell with study and bedroom, and a walled garden behind, with the front door of his cell opening out on to a broad cloister. At the side of the door was a hatch where his food would be left, twice a day, by a lay brother whom he never saw and never spoke to. A Carthusian monk was allowed to possess only a few things: pen, ink, books, razor, needle and thread, a white robe and a coarse shirt to irritate his flesh so that he might learn to accept hardship and privation cheerfully.

The day would be spent in prayer and meditation, and working in the garden, and the austerity of the Carthusian order was such that it was never in need of reform or improvement. The monks would meet in church for service each day but would not speak to one another. It was only on rare occasions that conversation was permitted, perhaps during an occasional communal meal, and then under the observation of the prior.

Because of the severity of the rule, the Carthusian order never became popular, and there were only nine Carthusian houses in England. The first of these was at Witham, in Somerset, of which practically nothing remains. Only at Mount Grace, in North Yorkshire, founded in 1398, is there a good layout of a Carthusian priory. It is an excellent example, including a rebuilt monk's cell in the cloister. Hinton, south of Bath, retains its chapter-house, while the London Charterhouse became Charterhouse School.

BLACK CANONS AND WHITE CANONS

The monasteries mentioned so far followed the Rule of St Benedict, with varied interpretations from one order to another. They were houses of monks whose lives were spent within the monastic communities. Two other types of monasteries existed, peopled by canons regular. These canons lived in communities, like the monks, but, unlike them, they went out preaching. Indeed, their monasteries served as centres of parochial activity, and their monks were

ORDER	TYPE OF COMMUNITY	FOUNDER	FIRST ENGLISH FOUND-ATION
BENEDICTINE	Monks or nuns	Named after, but not founded by, St Benedict, *c.*528	Battle Abbey, Sussex, 1087
CARTHUSIAN	Monks	St Bruno, 1084, at Grande Chartreuse	Witham Priory, Somerset, 1180–1
CISTERCIAN	Monks or nuns	Abbot Robert, Molesme, 1098. Re-formed by Abbot Stephen Harding 1109, implemented by Bernard of Clairvaux.	Waverley Abbey, Surrey, 1128
CLUNIAC	Monks or nuns	Duke of Aquitaine, at Cluny, 910	Lewes Priory, Sussex 1077
GILBERTINE	Canons or canons and nuns	St Gilbert of Sempringham, 1131	Sempringham, Lincs 1131
AUGUSTINIAN	Canons or canonesses	Named after, but not founded by, St Augustine of Hippo, *c.*423	St Botolph's Priory, Colchester, *c.*1093
PREMONS-TRATENSIAN	Canons or canonesses	St Norbert, at Prémontré, 1121	Newsham, Lincs 1143

ADMINISTRATION AND CHIEF CHARACTERISTICS	DRESS	APPROX. NO. OF HOUSES AT DISSOLUTION
Subject to episcopal authority, otherwise each abbey/priory reasonably autonomous. Major abbeys became wealthy. Monks studied, produced ecclesiastical biographies, monastic and national chronicles, works of art and scholarship.	Black habits, with cowls	282 + 92 nunneries
The most austere order. Main devotions, food taken, study and manual work all done in solitude in their cells and gardens. Communal service only on Sundays and holy days. Subject to papal authority.	Hair shirts and coarse clothing, white cloaks.	9
Initially austere, but later, as became wealthy, this was relaxed. Entensive use of lay brothers in farming and stock-breeding enterprises on vast estates. Annual chapter at Citeaux. Expansion through 'daughter houses'.	White habits with cowls. Black scapular over shoulders for church services.	80 + 29 nunneries
All priories subject ot Abbot of Cluny. Great emphasis on worship, liturgy, ceremonial, grandeur, but much of acquired wealth went to helping poor, needy, travellers and pilgrims.	Black habits	32
The only purely English order. Canons followed Augustinian rule, nuns the Benedictine. Lay brothers and lay sisters were also in the double houses. No intercommunications in monastery, but church services shared in sound not sight.	Canon – black habit, with white cloak. Nun _ black cloak and tunic, white cowl.	14 for canons only + 10 double houses
Canons not confined in monastic claustral life but could minister in appropriated parish churches. Episcopal authority. Some cathedral-priories. Augustinians founded many hospitals.	Black habits with cowl. White surplices, black cassocks.	170 + 23 nunneries
Tending to Cistercian interpretation of Augustinian rules. Centralised order under mother-house. Monasteries usually far from towns.	White habits	34 + 4 nunneries

BONSHOMMES	Brethen	Very similar to Augustinian. Only two houses at Ashridge (Herts) and Edington (Wilts).
BRIDGETTINE	Nuns and priests	Only one English house, 1415, subsequently moved to Syon Abbey (Middlesex).
GRANDMONTINE	Brethren	Another Benedictine offshoot. Three English houses: Albersbury (Shropshire), Craswell (Herefordshire), Grosmont (Yorks) – meagre remains at Craswell.
TIRONENSIAN	Congregation	Four English houses – Andwell and Hamble (Hants), St Cross (Wight), Titley (Herefordshire). See also Arbroath (Angus), Kelso (Scottish Borders) and St Dogmael's (Ceredigion)

priests who observed the Rule of St Augustine, Bishop of Hippo. They first appeared in England about 1100, when a community of Augustinians established itself at Colchester, where they built their monastery largely of available bricks from the old Roman town. Much of their church still stands, as St Botolph's Priory. The Augustinians were also known as the Austin Canons, and, wearing a black habit like the Benedictine monks, became called the Black Canons. Many of their splendid churches survive and are still in use, their large naves being evidence of the big congregations the Augustinians attracted, as at Bristol and Carlisle cathedrals, the priories of Bolton, Lanercost, Christchurch and Cartmel, and Dorchester Abbey. Generally, the Augustinians lived in comparative comfort, and certainly on a much more liberal scale than the monks, being especially generous in their hospitality.

A second order, following more austere ways of life, was formed at Premontre in France in 1123 and, being more akin to the Cistercians than the Benedictines, chose to wear a white habit. These Premonstratensians, more easily thought of as the White Canons, established their first English house at Alnwick in 1147 and eventually founded thirty-one abbeys and two nunneries throughout England. Only a few survive as ruins today, Easby (North Yorkshire), Egglestone (Durham), Shap (Cumbria), Titchfield (Hampshire) and Bayham (East Sussex) being the best.

The cloister court at Lacock Abbey in Wiltshire.

NUNS

During the middle ages there were over a hundred nunneries in England, but for the most part they were neither as wealthy nor as important as the bigger monasteries. They were usually small houses, and rather poor, mainly because the nuns could not undertake the type of farmwork which made the Cistercians wealthy, but also because they did not attract large gifts of money or land, except in the cases of Romsey in Hampshire and Barking in Essex.

Romsey Abbey, like most of the houses of nuns, was a Benedictine foundation, and its church is the finest of all the nuns' churches. The best remaining monastic buildings of a nunnery are those at Lacock Abbey in Wiltshire, which was a house of Augustinian canonesses, founded by the Countess Ela of Salisbury on the same day in 1232 as she also founded the Carthusian house at Hinton, 12 miles (19 km) to the west, south of Bath.

Most nunneries were priories, in the charge of a prioress, and under the overall rule of a monastery of the same order. Their inmates were very often women from quite well-to-do homes who had failed to find a husband. After some years as spinsters, and helping to bring up younger brothers and sisters, they were expected to 'take the veil' without particularly wanting to do so. In the nunnery, apart from the church services which they had to attend, nuns would spend much of their time weaving or spinning wool and linen for their

The parish church at Sempringham, Lincolnshire.

own clothes, and embroidering the church vestments. Rarely having been as well educated as men, they were not expected to spend much time in the cloisters reading and writing.

DOUBLE HOUSES

Gilbert of Sempringham, a twelfth-century Lincolnshire priest, was the only Englishman to found his own order. He established a convent for seven unmarried women of his parish, under Benedictine rule, spiritually ministered to by a small house of Augustinian canons. Lay brothers and lay sisters did manual work. Eventually, 26 Gilbertine double houses were founded, half of them during Gilbert's own lifetime. In them, canons and nuns had separate cloisters but worshipped together in one church, albeit with a wall high enough to prevent their seeing each other. These Gilbertine houses were ruled jointly by a prior and a prioress. Another similar order, the Bridgettines, had only one English house, Syon Abbey in Middlesex.

The officers of the monastery

✢ ✢ ✢ ✢ ✢ ✢

A community of monks or nuns living together is called a religious house or convent. A religious house of monks is a monastery, and of nuns a nunnery. Both monasteries and nunneries could be called abbeys or priories, the distinction being purely one of status. An abbey of monks would have as its head an abbot, one of nuns an abbess. A priory would have no resident abbot but would be presided over by a prior or prioress and in most cases was an offshoot from, and dependent upon, an abbey. Houses of regular canons living under monastic rule were also classified as abbeys or priories.

The *abbot* was the head of the monastery and was chosen by the monks themselves, for his goodness, his wisdom and his leadership. He had to be a father to the monks; his word was law and he had to be well educated in order to deal with all the wide range of monastic affairs and responsibilities. When, at first, the monasteries were small, the abbot lived, worked and even slept with his brother monks. But as monasteries grew in size and importance the abbot became a greater man, perhaps lord of one or more manors, a big landowner, and a friend of noblemen and even kings. By then it became necessary for him to have his own house within the precinct, the abbot's lodging, where he could entertain important guests and other monastic heads, although he did from time to time invite monks into his own house to join him at table.

Next in importance to the abbot was the *prior*. In a big monastery he would frequently have to take charge of affairs during the absences of the abbot; in the case of a priory he would be in complete charge, having been seconded to it from the mother abbey. The prior had an assistant called the *sub-prior*, and under him were the monks of the house who had special duties. These monks were called *obedientiaries*.

Each obedientiary had a specific job for which he was responsible. The church being the most important monastic building, the monk in charge of its services, called the *precentor*, would be the most important obedientiary. He made arrangements for all the services, was in charge of the music and the choir books, trained the monks to sing, decided the readings for the services and even had to provide materials for writing and repairing books from the choir and the cloister.

The *sacristan* looked after the contents of the church, the vestments worn, the valuable linen, the embroidered robes and banners, the gold and silver plate and the holy vessels of the altar. His chief helper, the *sub-sacristan*, had the extra responsibility of ringing the bell for each of the services throughout the day. Some monasteries possessed very valuable plate and holy relics, usually kept in a special container called the reliquary. Pilgrims sometimes travelled long distances to see these relics. At St Albans this reliquary and the nearby watching loft for the sacristan can still be seen.

The claustral life of the monastery was in the hands of a number of obedientiaries. The *cellarer* looked after the cellars and stores, housed in the undercroft, usually beneath the west range of the cloister. All the monastic supplies of food, ale and wines were stored there, in the cellarium. The best example of this building is the huge vaulted structure at Fountains Abbey. The cellarer would have to meet tradesmen, probably in the slype, which led from either the east or west side of the cloister, in order to buy or sell produce. He also looked after the bakehouse and the brewhouse, assisted by the *sub-cellarer*.

The *kitchener* was in charge of the kitchens, where the food was cooked, and the *fraterer*, or *refectorian*, looked after the serving of food in the frater, as well as seeing that clean towels were provided at the lavatorium, fresh rushes for the frater floor, and lamps during the dark days and evenings of winter. Servants waited on the monks in the frater.

The other buildings around the cloister were the responsibility of the *chamberlain*, whose job it was to see that the bedding in the monks' dorter was adequate and in good condition. He also had to provide the monks' habits, their boots and shoes and their linen. He also arranged the hot water supply for the washing of feet, usually on Saturdays, for the shaving of heads every three weeks, and baths perhaps once a quarter. In winter he had to see that the fire in the calefactory was kept well stoked up.

Monks who were old or sick lived in the infirmary, a separate building away from the cloister, but still within the precinct of the monastery. The *infirmarian* was in charge of this building, with its long room like a present-day hospital ward, having beds down each side. Sick monks were allowed to eat meat, something normally denied their more healthy brothers, and the infirmary's own dining-room was entirely separate from the main frater and was called the misericord.

Because they were constantly tending the sick, the infirmarian and his assistants gained considerable medical skill, a good knowledge of first aid and the ability to perform simple operations. As a result, lay people from outside came to the monasteries for treatment of illnesses, and payments for this would go towards providing better buildings. Medicines and ointments were made from herbs grown specially in the monastery herb garden.

In the Middle Ages many people were very poor, and one of the main tasks of a monastery was to help them. The *almoner* was responsible for this care of the poor, and he gave away scraps of food from the kitchen, worn clothing and other materials to the folk who queued up each day for their 'dole'. Some monasteries fed an exact number of people each day, giving them perhaps 'a mess of pottage [peas and beans], a farthing loaf, and a farthingsworth of beer'.

The cellars in the west range of Fountains Abbey, Yorkshire.

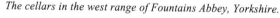

Evesham Abbey, Worcestershire: the almonry building is now a museum.

The *hospitaller*, or *guest-master*, dispensed hospitality to the many visitors and pilgrims who came to the monastery. Such travellers would be given a bed and a meal in the guest-house, or, if they were poor, in the almonry. In either case, they were not expected to pay unless they wanted to, since the monastery regarded hospitality to wayfarers as part of its duty. Important guests would be entertained in the abbot's lodging. Care of travellers even extended in some cases to the provision and upkeep of roads leading to the monastery.

The *master of the novices* was the monk in charge of the boys and young men who were learning to become monks. First, a *novice* would have the top of his head shaved bare – the 'tonsure'; then he received his habit, a long robe with wide sleeves and a hood (black for Benedictines, white for Cistercians). Preparation for monkhood and lessons in the cloisters would last at least a year for the young men, and more for boys, and after it the novice would make his vows, of poverty, obedience and chastity. Then he would get his monk's cowl (a very big hood) and would be one of the monks of the convent or religious house.

The layout of a monastery

✣ ✣ ✣ ✣ ✣ ✣

BUILDING OPERATIONS

In medieval times the monastic ideal of life was regarded as of the highest importance. As a result, there was rarely a shortage of funds to pay for the building of the monasteries or for their endowment. Income came chiefly from the possessions of the chapter, in land, property and benefices. Offerings made at the altar and at saints' shrines often amounted to a considerable sum, while miracle-working relics and roods, such as St Edmund's bones at Bury St Edmunds and the roods at Malmesbury and Bermondsey, brought numerous gifts.

The early monasteries were erected very largely by the monks themselves but it was not long before their design and building passed into the more capable hands of professional lay craftsmen. As with any major building, an architect, called the master mason, was appointed to take overall control. Decisions about position, size and style of building would initially need the approval of the abbot or prior, who, with the sacrist, would also handle the financial aspect. But the work itself and the employment of itinerant masons and other craftsmen was the responsibility of the master mason. Rough masons worked the big stone blocks and reduced them to a manageable size. More highly paid and very much more skilled freemasons handled the freestone, working with mallet and chisel; they moulded the arches, cut the delicate tracery and did much of the carving. Individual gifted monks also undertook the skilled work of carving, but most of the work was in lay hands. As an example of cost, the eastern half of Westminster Abbey, built between 1245 and 1269, cost King Henry III £50,000.

A STANDARD PLAN

By 1066 the layout of all monasteries of monks and canons had become standardised. Within the basic plan there were some small but regular differences between the houses of the Black Monks and those of the White Monks, while the Carthusians were exceptionally different. In addition, differences of siting between the various monasteries brought about local variations in the basic plan. Monastic plans in Britain followed the continental pattern and not the old English one. Any Saxon monasteries remaining at the Norman Conquest were pulled down and replaced by bigger and grander structures.

The essential parts of the monastic plan were the great church, the claustral buildings around which the monks lived, the buildings where they looked after their sick and showed hospitality to guests, and the curia, or great court, in whose buildings were carried out the day-to-day administration of the monastery and its estates, and where it also made contact with the outside world.

The medieval arrangement of these four main parts of a monastery showed a Norman genius for planning in that it was both practical and quite simple. The church stood on the highest ground, its nave forming one side of a quadrangle called the cloister. Round the other three sides of this cloister were the buildings (the 'claustral' buildings) where the monks lived, ate and slept. The administrative buildings, and those where outside contact was made, were grouped in the outer courtyard – the 'curia' – west of the cloister; the infirmary lay to the east, in the quietest and most peaceful part of the site. The complete layout was usually enclosed by a precinct wall, entry through which was by one or more gatehouses. Whenever a monastery was built, the church was built first, starting at the east end with the high altar and the monks' quire, together with the eastern range of the cloister, including the chapter-house and monks' dormitory.

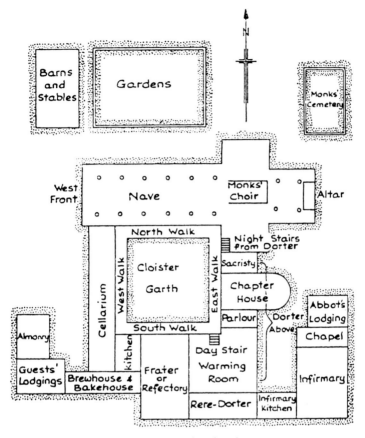

Sketch plan of a typical medieval monastery.

THE CHURCH

As it was the building round which the monastery grew, and the place in which more than half the waking hours of the monks were spent in the service of God, the church was the most important building of the monastery. In all but the very smallest monasteries the church was planned in the form of a cross – a 'cruciform' shape. This consisted of, from east to west, a presbytery, a choir, transepts (often with chapels on their eastern sides) and a nave. The presbytery housed the high altar and was for important ceremonies connected with it. The transepts were mainly for movement and communication. The nave was for the use of servants, lay brothers (in Cistercian monasteries) and, in many cases, for the local laity of the adjoining parish.

Norman presbyteries were not very long, extending to two, three or four bays, and ending in an apse. They would usually have an aisle on each side, this aisle being continued round the back of the apse to form a processional path, as at Gloucester, Norwich, Tewkesbury and St Bartholomew's, Smithfield, in London. As church ceremonial developed to include magnificent choral masses and services specially in honour of the Virgin Mary, special chapels were built for this purpose, called Lady Chapels. Usually these were added on to the east end of the presbytery, as at Gloucester, Winchester and Christchurch, but special conditions sometimes demanded their building on to the west end, as at Durham and Glastonbury.

These more elaborate presbyteries were suitable only for the larger abbey churches. Smaller buildings had square-ended presbyteries with either very short aisles or no aisles at all. The Benedictines had no aisle in the priory at Lindisfarne, nor had the Augustinians at Bolton Priory or the Premonstratensians at Easby Abbey.

The churches of all Cistercian monasteries were dedicated to the Virgin Mary, so they did not need Lady Chapels. The earlier ones were structurally as simple as a cruciform plan could be, with a short aisleless presbytery, short transepts with rectangular chapels on the east and an aisleless nave. These very short presbyteries of early Cistercian simplicity are represented at Kirkstall and Valle Crucis.

However, as Cistercian austerity gradually relaxed during the twelfth century, the shape of the presbytery developed and grew. At Abbey Dore there was an aisled presbytery of three bays, with a row of five chapels beyond it. The extended presbytery became the pride of the great northern abbeys of all orders: Augustinian Thornton had six bays, Benedictine Whitby and Cistercian Rievaulx had seven bays, Augustinian Carlisle and Kirkham had eight bays, while Benedictine York went to nine. Cistercian Fountains added to its aisled presbytery of five bays a spectacular eastern transept, later copied by Durham, and famous at both places as the Chapel of the Nine Altars.

St Mary's Abbey, York: the remains of the church walls and the crossing-tower.

Binham Priory, Norfolk: the nave of the priory church is now the parish church.

The choir lay to the west of the presbytery, usually filling the space of the crossing and the first eastern bays of the nave – still apparent at Gloucester and Westminster. This monks' choir was separated from the nave by a double screen with a central doorway, and altars on each side of this on the western face. The screen was called the pulpitum, and from it the epistle and gospel would be read at certain times; the organ was often situated above it. Norwich has a restored pulpitum of stone, while Hexham has a splendid wooden one.

The monks' stalls faced each other along both sides of the choir, and on each side of the pulpitum doorway, with the abbot sitting on the south side of the doorway and the prior on the north.

The transept nearest to the cloister (usually the south one) usually contained the night stairs leading to the adjoining monks' dormitory (dorter), thus making for easy access for the monks to the church for services in the night hours. Few complete examples of night stairs have survived, and by far the best is at Hexham. Traces of the night stairs can be identified at various monastic ruins, for example at Rievaulx. Cluniac monasteries such as Castle Acre, Thetford and Wenlock dispensed with night stairs completely, so that there was no direct communication between the monks' dormitory and the church.

The nave of the church was always built last. Sometimes it took so long that the style of the building changed, from Norman to early Gothic, before the job was finished, as at Peterborough, Romsey and Selby. In the greater abbey churches of both Benedictine and Cistercian foundation the nave was often very long – seven bays at Buildwas and Blyth, eight at Durham and Roche, nine at Binham and Rievaulx, ten at St Albans and Furness, eleven at Fountains and Peterborough, twelve bays at Byland and Winchester, and at Norwich it reached to fourteen bays. Cistercian naves were long in order to house the lay brothers. In Benedictine churches and those of the Augustinian canons the nave was open for lay people, and in some cases where the rest of the church was destroyed at

Malmesbury Abbey, Wiltshire: the decoration on the south porch.

the Dissolution this parochial use of the nave, or even of an aisle, helped to keep it in use. This has occurred at Binham, Bridlington, Dunstable, Elstow, Nun Monkton and Tynemouth, to name a few, while at Romsey, Leominster, Tewkesbury, Blyth and Cartmel a separate aisle was provided for the lay folk of the parish.

For special processions on church festivals the west door of the nave would be used. Only a few monasteries were without this entrance: these included Cartmel, Buildwas, Furness and Romsey. Most of them possessed in addition to this western portal another doorway to the nave, for lay use, near the west end of the church on the opposite side to the cloister. This doorway often had a porch to protect it, the most splendid example being that at Malmesbury, showing superb Norman carving. Later examples can be seen at Canterbury, Chester, Great Malvern and Gloucester.

Most monastic churches were graced by the addition of towers, either a single one over the crossing, or two, one at the crossing and one at the west end of the nave, or even three, with two at the west. Early central towers were always low ones, as at Winchester, Buildwas and Romsey. Subsequent ones were surmounted by rather squat pyramidal roofs, and in later years the towers were built higher (but not always on the best foundations, many collapsing as a result) at Bourne, Bridlington and Worksop, where, in each case, the west tower survived. Evesham built a separate tower to house the bells in the early sixteenth century, and this detached structure still stands. Early Cistercian churches were forbidden towers as being too decorative and elaborate, and not in keeping with Cistercian ideals, but as these ideals became relaxed towers were constructed. Most stately of them is that built by Abbot Huby at Fountains about 1500, erected at the end of the north transept because the central tower was beginning to collapse.

Many monasteries possessed shrines housing the relics of saints. Best-known are those of St Thomas à Becket at Canterbury, St Cuthbert at Durham and St Edward the Confessor at Westminster. The shrines were normally given a position of honour, behind the high altar and near the entrance to the Lady Chapel.

The layout of a monastery

Winchester Cathedral with its low central tower.

FRIARS' CHURCHES

By the beginning of the thirteenth century, when Cistercian austerity was waning, there was little difference in either plan or elevation between the abbey churches of the Benedictine and Cistercian orders. But the friars, whose main duty of preaching distinguished them from the monks and canons, built large churches specially for that purpose. These churches had naves with wide aisles and broad arcades, and choirs which were without aisles, although very long.

THE CLOISTERS

Although architecturally the church was the grandest building in the monastery and was its spiritual centre, representing the main reason for its existence as a monastery, the cloister and its associated buildings deserve the fullest study, so that the monks can be seen in the framework of their own society. The monks' vows of poverty, obedience and chastity shut them off from the world and confined them within the cloister garth or lawn and its immediate surroundings.

The position of the cloister in relation to the church depended on the lie of the land and the direction of the nearest flowing water for drainage. Ideally, the site for a Cistercian or Premonstratensian monastery would be one on rising ground to the north of a river or stream flowing from west to east. These conditions were obtained naturally at Fountains, and artificially at Dryburgh. Where conditions did allow, the cloister was placed on the south side of the nave of the church, to catch the sun, and to avoid being in the shadow of the roofs of high buildings. The awkward position of the river at Tintern and Buildwas caused the cloister to be built to the north of the church. Many Benedictine abbeys were

Tintern Abbey, Monmouthshire: the collation seat in the south walk of the cloister.

situated in towns, very rarely being on virgin sites. Hence they showed planning idiosyncrasies, too, and north-side cloisters exist at Canterbury, Chester, Gloucester and Bury St Edmunds. At Rochester the cloister is even against the eastern arm of the nave.

Each of the four sides of the cloister had a covered alley of one storey, with a lean-to type of roof against the adjoining wall of the church or other building. Early cloisters had open arcades along the side facing the garth, standing on low walls. Small reconstructed portions of these arcades can be seen at Rievaulx and Newminster. Cloisters built after the introduction of tracery had their open arcades replaced by windows, the later ones being glazed.

Cloisters served many purposes. Primarily they were galleries of communication between the various domestic buildings themselves, and between them and the church. The cloister alley next to the church wall was the recognised place for meditation, and the monks would spend their allotted periods of prayer, reading, study and meditation in that alley. Some cloisters had stone benches along the church wall for the monks to sit on. The outer wall of this alley was divided into carrels, each carrel occupying the space of half a window. Carrels were separated from one another by wainscoting and contained a desk for books. Carrels can be seen at Gloucester and Chester.

A rare Cistercian survival associated with these study periods, particularly with the Collation, the evening reading before Compline, is the abbot's seat against the church wall halfway along the cloister alley nearest to the church. Cleeve possesses the best example of the arched recess for the abbot's chair, while Tintern has an easily identifiable one.

The range of buildings adjoining the eastern alleyway of the cloister was usually of two storeys, all of the upper floor forming the dorter, or monks' dormitory, with a doorway leading to the night stairs in the nearby transept. Few

Kirkham Priory, Yorkshire: the latrine channel.

dorters still retain their floors and roofs, and those which do are now used for other purposes: at Durham and Westminster they house libraries, and at Cleeve and Valle Crucis they were converted for domestic use by later inhabitants.

The reredorter or necessarium (latrine block) of the monastery was placed at the end of the dorter furthest from the church, usually jutting out at right angles from the dorter, or extending across its end, as at Lewes and Castle Acre. Its position was governed by the course of the main drain, which was channelled along a walled-in course, often constructed with fine masonry, as it was of great importance. Above this drain, carrying running water, the reredorter was a long narrow building with a row of stone seats against the wall, each with a window, and divided from the next by a partition. If the dorter was in an unusual position, as at Easby and Worcester, where it was in the western range of buildings, this was due entirely to the need to place it in the position most convenient for the main drain. This influence of drainage on the monastic layout is best seen at Kirkham, where the drain follows a quarter circle south-east of the cloister, and a long crescent of buildings – reredorter, kitchens, prior's lodging and infirmary – follows its course.

THE CHAPTER-HOUSE

The chapter-house was the most important of the eastern range of buildings, regarded as second in importance to the church. The dormitory ran either above it or above its entrance lobby. Early chapter-houses were regarded as sufficiently sacred for the burial of abbots. The twelfth-century chapter-house at Rievaulx is unique in containing the shrine of the first abbot, William, erected a century after his death. No other English chapter-house contains such a treasure.

The name 'chapter-house' comes from the fact that after each daily Morrow Mass at 8 a.m. the monks assembled there for a sort of business meeting, which

Wenlock Priory, Shropshire: the Norman arcading in the chapter-house.

began with a reading that always included a chapter from St Benedict's Rules. This would be followed by lists of the daily and weekly duties of monks. Obituaries of the day and confessions of faults would be heard, and resultant punishments decreed. In addition, the temporal business of the monastery would be carried out in the chapter-house.

Because they were so important, chapter-houses were often constructed with great architectural dignity and elegance, this elaboration being shown at Bristol and Wenlock by rows of beautiful internal arcading. There are other good examples at Hinton Charterhouse, Chester, Haughmond and Furness, with polygonal ones at Westminster, Worcester, Cockersand and Margam.

The ground floor of the dorter range was usually divided into a number of rooms, each leading on to the cloister. The slype came nearest to the transept. This was a passage leading through the range to the east of the church, where the monks' cemetery was sited. This passage sometimes served the purpose of a parlour, where limited conversation could take place. Elsewhere, the ground floor had to contain the day stairs, by which the monks could reach their dormitory during daylight, the warming-house, with its one or more fireplaces, and a passage to the infirmary quarters. In Cistercian monasteries the warming-house was situated near the refectory, as at Fountains and Tintern.

THE FRATER RANGE

The frater range flanked the alleyway directly opposite the church, except in Cistercian monasteries, where, instead of running parallel to the cloister alley, it was at right angles to it. The frater, or refectory, was the monks' dining-hall, and internally it was similar to any medieval great hall. The entrance to it from the cloister was at its western end. Near this doorway, and along the cloister wall, was the lavatorium (lavatory), where the monks washed their hands before going in to eat. This lavatory was usually a long stone trough set back into the frater wall of the cloister, as at Rievaulx and Fountains. At Haughmond and

Kirkham it was in the west wall, and at Gloucester it was in the low inner cloister wall below the windows. Wenlock, Exeter and Canterbury are among the few English examples which followed the continental system of having a separate little pavilion centrally placed in the cloister garth, its basin fed by a pipe.

The monastic refectories of Chester, Cleeve and Worcester survive, while that of Beaulieu is now used as the parish church. In the refectory hall the tables would be parallel to the side walls, with the high table at the east end, where the chief monastic officers ate. There may have been a reredos behind this high table, and on a side wall close to it there was a pulpit from which one of the monks read aloud during meals. This reader's pulpit was reached by a stairway in the thickness of the wall, examples of this occurring at Chester, Fountains, Shrewsbury and Beaulieu.

The eating of meat, but not bird flesh, was forbidden but as this observance, like so many others, was relaxed, particularly for sick brethren, special permission to eat meat was granted, but it had to be done in a room other than the refectory. So at some monasteries second dining-halls were built, smaller than the main one, and called 'misericords'.

In Benedictine monasteries kitchens were built near the refectories, but standing free from them on the side away from the cloister. As at Easby and Castle Acre, the kitchen was normally rectangular; at Durham it was polygonal. The fine and complete abbot's kitchen survives at Glastonbury, a square building with fireplaces diagonally in the angles, and arches carrying an octagonal vaulted roof.

Cistercian kitchens were near the cloister, placed so that meals prepared there could be served to the monks in the refectory and to the lay brothers in their building. At Fountains the fireplaces were placed back to back in the centre of the kitchen, a door into the cloister near at hand simplifying the task of getting provisions from the great cellar.

Beaulieu Abbey, Hampshire: the monk's pulpit in the former frater, now the parish church.

Glastonbury Abbey, Somerset: the abbot's kitchen is one of the best preserved medieval kitchens in Europe.

The cellarium, or cellar, was the great storehouse of the monastery and formed the western range of the claustral buildings. As the outer court, or curia, through which provisions would enter the monastery, lay to the west, there is an obvious and practical reason for having the cellar in this western range, that of giving direct access. The cellar was usually the basement or undercroft of this western range, stone-vaulted from a row of central columns. At Fountains, the superb cellar has twenty-two bays and is double-aisled, part used as a store and a smaller part as a parlour between cloister and outer court.

In some of the Cistercian abbeys the upper floor of this western range formed a dormitory for the lay brothers, as at Fountains, and in some Cistercian and Benedictine monasteries it was divided into a number of rooms, for the head of the convent and for guests, together with, possibly, a chapel and also a common hall for servants of the monastery. Sometimes, where unorthodox arrangements had been forced upon the monastery through an awkward lie of the land, as at Durham and Easby, the monks' dorter occupied this upper floor of the cellar range.

THE ABBOT'S AND GUESTS' LODGINGS

An abbot's quarters were similar to those of any other medieval lord, either ecclesiastical or lay. It must be remembered that the abbot of a great monastery was as important a patron of architecture as a great nobleman or a bishop, so the development of the design of his quarters, and those of his guests, was comparable to that of the big halls of medieval castles.

When the abbot's rooms were above the cellar range, they consisted of a hall, a chapel and two or three other chambers. When, as occurred more often, they were not in this position, there was no particular site allotted for them. At Castle Acre and Chester they were in a wing abutting on to the range nearest the church. At Easby the abbot's lodging was north of the church, and at Haughmond it was south of the cloisters; the priors of Tynemouth and Lindisfarne had quarters near the south end of the dorter range, as, later, did the prior of Bolton. At Norwich the guests were above the cellar range, and the bishop developed his own palace north of the church. Cistercian abbots tended to have lodgings south of the cloister, usually as a detached building, as at Rievaulx and Fountains (which, oddly, had prisoners' cells beneath it). One of the most characteristic examples of abbot's lodgings is at Roche, complete with its hall, kitchen, buttery, pantry and other chambers.

Fountains retained two early examples of guest-houses as separate buildings a short way from the monastery, each of them having two floors, with each floor unequally divided into hall and chamber. Bardney and Kirkstall have aisled halls with chambers in cross-wings, and Kirkstall later grew to have its guest-houses as a complete self-contained unit round a small courtyard, with kitchen and stables.

Castle Acre Priory, Norfolk: the west front of the church and the prior's lodgings.

Boxgrove Priory, Sussex: the ruins of the guest-house.

THE INFIRMARY RANGE

Sick monks, and those whose advancing years made them unable to cope with the severity of claustral life, were housed in the infirmary, which usually stood east of the cloister, thus being well away from any noise from the outer court to the west. Basically, it consisted of a hall, a chapel and a kitchen providing a more appropriate diet than the normal monastic one. Some infirmaries had a special little frater of their own in which it was permitted to eat meat. The infirmarian also had two or three rooms as his own quarters.

The infirmaries of Benedictine monasteries were arranged rather like a church in plan, the hall being equivalent to the nave, the inmates' beds occupying

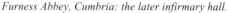

Furness Abbey, Cumbria: the later infirmary hall.

Thornton Abbey, Lincolnshire: the largest monastic gatehouse in Britain.

the 'aisles', and the infirmary chapel where the chancel would be, preferably correctly orientated west-east, like those of Peterborough, Ely and Canterbury.

Cistercian infirmaries developed to become a set of buildings grouped round its own little cloister, as at Rievaulx and Tintern. Fountains had a huge infirmary hall, 180 feet (55 metres) long by 80 feet (24 metres) wide, some of the columns of which still stand. Its chapel, kitchen and infirmarian's house lay to the east. In sharp contrast, Premonstratensian infirmaries did not have chapels at all. Some Cistercian ones, Roche and Jervaulx among them, had a second infirmary for the lay brothers.

THE OUTER COURT

The buildings of the outer court, that is, those not associated or connected with the church or the claustral buildings, were essentially those concerned with the running of a self-contained community. Their number and size depended on the size of the monastery, which could vary from, say, twenty inmates of a small priory to perhaps six or seven hundred in a big Cistercian abbey such as Rievaulx.

Most of the outer court buildings were probably timber-framed, so very few have survived. Foundation plans help to give us a picture: at Fountains, for example, brewhouses and bakehouses can be identified, and the mill is still working. In addition to these, which were common to all monasteries, there would be an almonry (where charity was dispensed), a granary – and barns for storing the different types of grain, workshops (a big monastery like Durham or Norwich would have a permanent masons' shop, carpenters' workshop, and probably a draughtsman's room), a smithy, a slaughterhouse, a hen-house, separate buildings for oxen, cows, calves and pigs, and a dovecote for the monastic pigeons, although this was more likely to have been built on higher ground outside the monastic precincts, as at Bruton, Somerset, the ruins of whose dovecote stand very conspicuously to the south of the town.

Monastic precincts were entered through the main gatehouse, a building almost invariably at least two storeys high. The ground floor was taken up by the passage through the gatehouse, with archways front and back, broad ones for wheeled traffic, and smaller side arches for foot traffic. Easby and Worksop have these two arches, of different sizes, in cross-walls in the middle of the gate passage. The porter who controlled movements through the gatehouse had access by a small doorway in one of the side walls.

Ely Priory, Cambridgeshire: the Ely Porta or south gatehouse.

Many gatehouses still stand; indeed, at Kingswood (Gloucestershire) and Montacute (Somerset) they are the only monastic remains. Size varies greatly: Kingswood's is small and gabled, contrasting with the massive and handsome gatehouses at Thornton, Battle, St Albans and Bury St Edmunds. The upper floors at Ely and St Albans contained prisons; those at York and Whalley were chapels. Monasteries with very extensive precincts had more than one gatehouse; Bury St Edmunds had four, two of which still stand, as do the two at St Augustine's at Canterbury. Furness Abbey also had two on the precinct wall, one outside and a fourth inside leading to the monks' cemetery. Tintern and York had additional gatehouses leading to nearby rivers, and these were naturally called watergates.

Some Benedictine monasteries had parish churches on, or very near, the line of the precinct wall. Where this occurred, the gatehouse was built close to the church, as at Reading and Abingdon, and in each of these instances there was also a lay infirmary next door, dedicated to John the Baptist, and under abbey administration. Cistercian abbeys, having naves for lay brothers and thus not serving parish purposes, frequently provided a special lay chapel outside the precinct wall. A number of these have survived through becoming parish churches after the Dissolution, as at Kirkstead, Little Coggeshall, Merevale, Rievaulx and Tilty.

OUTSIDE THE PRECINCT

Many monastic buildings lay beyond the monastery's walls, and these were usually concerned with its provisioning and the running of its estates. Huge amounts of fish were needed for the monks, so, wherever they could, monasteries acquired fishing rights in both sea and fresh waters. St Dogmael's had the rights on the river Teifi; Chester had a boat on the river Dee, and another, with ten nets, off Anglesey. In the low-lying lands of mid Somerset, at Meare, Glastonbury Abbey built the fourteenth-century fish house as the home, workplace and store of the abbot's fisherman, whose job it was to look after the abbey fisheries, which were centred on the 300 acre (121 hectare) Meare Pool. Nearby is the Manor Farm, built at the same time as the fish house, as a summer home for the abbot of Glastonbury, while Saighton Grange in Cheshire fulfilled the same

Glastonbury Abbey, Somerset: the abbot's fish house at Meare.

purpose for the abbots of Chester.

Granges were monastic farms. The biggest ones, like that of Minster-in-Thanet, were almost miniature monasteries. The well-known village of Grange-in-Borrowdale in the Lake District was once the site of the 'grange farm' of the monks of Furness Abbey, who farmed much of that valley from 1211 to the Dissolution.

Monasteries were great landowners, either of lands close to the abbeys themselves, as at Glastonbury, Abbotsbury and Whitby, or of more outlying possessions. For example, the abbess of Shaftesbury, in Dorset, held much land in Wiltshire, the produce of which was stored in the great medieval barns at Tisbury and Bradford-on-Avon.

Tisbury tithe barn, Wiltshire, belonged to the abbess of Shaftesbury and is the largest in Britain.

Walsingham Abbey, Norfolk: the Slipper Chapel.

Monasteries, especially those with shrines, attracted many medieval pilgrims. Roadside chapels were built for them, the most outstanding being the Slipper Chapel near Walsingham. A lesser-known and quite humble one is at Chapel Plaister, north of Bradford-on-Avon, for pilgrims bound for Glastonbury. At Glastonbury is the famous George and Pilgrims Inn, where they could stay, while Gloucester and Canterbury also have fine inns for medieval pilgrims to the abbeys. One unusual survival, also at Glastonbury, is the Abbot's Tribunal, the building where the abbot held his court and dealt with legal matters connected with his vast estates.

CHARTERHOUSES

Carthusian priories, by the very nature of the rigidly austere rule of their order, differed in many ways from those of the other orders already described. Of the nine Carthusian priories founded in England, Mount Grace, in North Yorkshire, offers the best opportunity to study the layout, almost in its entirety.

The Carthusian plan necessitated there being at least two courtyards in the arrangements. The outer one, entered through a gatehouse, contained the usual buildings associated with an outer court: stables, barns and a guest-house, which at Mount Grace, became a private house in 1654. This outer court led to a very tiny court, containing the cells of the prior and the sacrist, the chapter-house on the east and, next to it, the aisleless presbytery of the small plain church. This range of buildings, together with the frater for use only on occasional days, separated the outer court from the large cloister garth to the north, of which it formed the south side.

This great cloister, at Mount Grace, is not square. Its north-west side is 272 feet (83 metres) and the other three are 231 feet (70 metres) each; no sides are parallel and no angles equal! The separate cells of the monks were small, two-storeyed cottages placed at intervals round this great cloister. Each cell was 27 feet (8.2 metres) square, with a doorway leading on to the cloister. Inside, the ground floor was divided to give a living-room, bedroom, study and small oratory, while the upper floor was used as a workshop. As the monk ate most of his meals alone, he received his food through an L-shaped hatch in the cottage wall facing the cloister garth. It was this shape so that the server from the kitchen and the monk inside could not see each other. Each cell had a piped water supply and stood inside its own walled garden, at the far end of which was a tiny privy, outlet from which was to a continuous drain running round the outside of the claustral buildings.

The arrangement of the single cells, one of which has been reconstructed at

Mount Grace, allowed the Carthusian monks not only to dwell apart from the world, but also to live a hermit-like existence apart from one another. Refectory meals were eaten only on Sundays and festivals, and the Carthusian monk would attend church only once or twice each day. The rest of his time he would spend alone in his cell or working in his little garden.

In the London charterhouse there are some remains of cell doorways and service hatches. Hinton Charterhouse is a village and Carthusian monastery a few miles south of Bath, where the finest remains are those of the chapter-house, perfectly preserved. The site of the two cloisters has been shown by excavation.

FRIARIES

The houses of friars differed again from those of the other orders, primarily because they were more like missionary headquarters than permanent homes. They were mostly in towns, where they were built a long time after the towns had taken shape. Thus the friaries were situated on any spare plot of land, in poor-quality buildings, sometimes little more than wooden huts, and often without a chapel. As both the Dominican and Franciscan friars became more numerous, their orders tended to adopt the more usual form of monastic layout, albeit distinctly simplified: church (large nave for preaching, small choir), small cloister, chapter-house, dorter and frater. The cloister was not used for study and therefore was reduced to a single corridor; choir and nave were separated by a narrow passage beneath a slender tower; and the main entrance lay to the north of the church. Most friaries vanished at the Dissolution; only the larger churches, such as Norwich, Chichester and the City of London, remained.

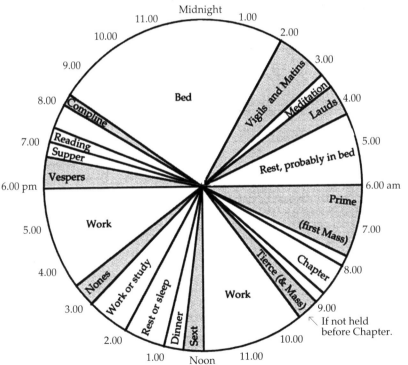

The monks' day (horarium), based on the Fountains Abbey Horarium. The main church services, held communally, are shaded. The diagram is only an approximation, and the activities would vary seasonally. In winter, hours for sleep would be increased, and opportunities made for monks to warm themselves in the warming-house.

The daily life

✣ ✣ ✣ ✣ ✣ ✣

A monk's day was divided up, not by mealtimes like our day is, but by the services of the church. There were eight of these and, with variations from summer to winter and from one order to another, the basic framework of the monk's day was built round these services. It started and finished much earlier than ours – a monk would rise about 2 a.m. and go to bed about 6.30 p.m. in the winter and 8 p.m. in summer.

Three of the eight church services occurred before daybreak – Matins shortly after rising, followed by Lauds and Prime, the monks remaining in the church throughout this time, although in some orders monks were allowed back in their dormitories between Lauds and Prime. Three of the services were held during the day, at intervals of three hours, the services being called Tierce, Sext and None (three, six and nine). The other two services, Vespers and Compline, were held at sunset and just before bedtime.

After Prime, say between 7 a.m. and 8 a.m., was the time when monks read or meditated in the cloisters, before going up the day stairs to their dormitory to exchange their night shoes for their day shoes, returning to the cloister to wash, and then going into church again. Some monks would be excused service so that they could carry on with some of the essential monastery business, such as helping in the refectory or preparing to read there during the main meal of the day.

Tierce was the first daily service, and this was followed by Mass, during which lay people were allowed into the nave of the church. After Mass came the daily Chapter, held in the chapter-house, and attended only by the monks from that particular religious house, presided over by the abbot, or, if he was away, by the prior.

Chapter, then, was a private meeting, held behind locked doors, at which the temporal business of the monastery would be discussed. Psalms, collects and the day's martyrology were read, followed by the abbot's sermon. Any monkish misdemeanours would then be reported to the abbot or prior, confessions heard, and punishments, where merited, would be meted out. Some of these were very harsh, and Benedictine and Cistercian rule allowed for corporal punishment to be administered, a birch rod being used.

Chapter would last until about 10 a.m. and was followed by a period of work until noon, when the monks returned to church for Sext, with High Mass immediately afterwards. Then came the first – and main – meal of the day, held in the refectory, or frater. This would be presided over by the abbot, prior or senior monk, seated at high table on a raised dais at the upper end of the room. During the meal the day's reader would go into the pulpit at the side of the room and read from a chosen work.

In Cistercian houses this main meal, dinner, consisted of a pound of bread and two courses of vegetables, probably cooked without fat. In Benedictine monasteries, and in Cistercian ones later on, when rules became more relaxed, all sorts of fish, pastry, vegetables, cheese, wines and milk were set before the monks. At special festivals there would also be pork pies and capons, blancmange and fruit tarts, and, as time went on, menus started to include poultry, salmon, eels, sides of beef or mutton, venison, oysters, spiced vegetables, butter and eggs.

After dinner most monks studied or worked until Nones, held between 2 p.m. and 3 p.m., and then until Vespers. In houses other than Cistercian ones, servants and peasant labour carried out the manual tasks in the monastery, as well as working in the garden or on the farm lands, thus leaving the monks themselves to concentrate on reading or writing, carving or painting, or tending the sick in the monastery's infirmary. Young monks and novices were even allowed the recreation offered by a game of bowls or skittles.

Vespers would be sung in church about 6 p.m., or earlier in winter, followed by a very light supper of bread and fruit, with a drink of ale. Night shoes, which were warmer than day shoes, would by now have been put on, and the monks would be summoned by the church bell to the last service of the day, Compline, after which they would return to their dorter in procession and retire to bed until roused again by the bell for Matins, when they would descend by the night stairs to the church for the daily round of church services again.

On fast days and throughout Lent the rule of all orders permitted only one meal a day, and that in the evening. The monastic rules were worked out either in Italy or in France for the conditions which obtained there, and they were not altered to allow for the harsher conditions of the more northern latitudes in Britain. A monk's life was a hard and very strict one, and it is quite remarkable that the whole story of Britain's monasteries is not largely one of attempts to evade the rule, and the punishments which ensued. The monastic discipline not only survived throughout four and a half centuries but succeeded in producing men of great wisdom and learning, having both intellectual and spiritual power, men whose leadership and guidance helped to shape history.

Throughout the middle ages monasteries were not only centres of religious and civilised life but served the community around them as church, hospital, school, library, farm, business centre and inn. Spiritual fortresses in a savage world they were most certainly, but they were not all, and not always, the islands of quiet sanctity their present appearances might suggest. The bigger monasteries in particular must have been full of interesting activity.

MONASTERIES AND THE LANDSCAPE

The extent to which monasteries in the Middle Ages helped to change the landscape is not often realised. In the twelfth and thirteenth centuries much marsh and fen land in Lincolnshire, Somerset and Kent was reclaimed by the monasteries of Peterborough, Ely, Croyland, Glastonbury, Muchelney, Athelney and Canterbury Cathedral Priory. The reclaimed marshes then carried thousands of sheep, but even these flocks were only a fraction of those run by the Cistercian monasteries on the northern hills and moors, and on the wolds and downlands of the southern counties. The French abbey of Caen had 1500 sheep grazing Minchinhampton Common in the Cotswolds; Fountains owned at least 15,000 sheep on the Pennines, Rievaulx almost as many on the Yorkshire Moors, Tintern over 2000 on Welsh hills, and Neath over 4000, all in the thirteenth century. Sheep farming on this scale followed almost ranch-like lines and was operated from the many granges which were built by the Cistercians on their outlying estates. Boundary walls were built to separate the monastic estates, and these medieval walls formed the basis of the later walls, many of which still delineate the upland landscapes of the Yorkshire Dales and of Wales. Cistercians also cleared many woodlands in fertile vales, such as the Vale of York, where arable granges were established.

In some parts of Britain monastic buildings would be a common and a grand sight. By 1350, the heyday of monastic building, there were probably at least eight hundred monasteries of various orders and sizes. In Yorkshire alone there were sixty-six, and in Lincolnshire fifty-one, with over forty each in Kent, Somerset and Gloucestershire. The number of monks, nuns and canons at this time probably exceeded 15,000, but this quickly started to fall after the middle of the fourteenth century, for it was from then that the Cistercian lay brothers vanished from the scene.

The Dissolution

✢ ✢ ✢ ✢ ✢ ✢

There was a slow decline in the number of monasteries from the middle of the fourteenth century onwards. Anglo-French wars had contributed to this in that they created obvious difficulties of communication between the parent abbeys in France (Citeaux, Cluny and Premontre) with their daughter foundations in England of the Cistercian, Cluniac and Premonstratensian orders. The Cluniacs suffered most in this respect, and a number had forcibly become independent priories.

By the fifteenth century many small houses had simply become too inadequate to exist, especially some of the Augustinian canons, and they just faded out. Longleat in Wiltshire was one example, and its lands were handed over to the Carthusians at Hinton. Some small and inefficient priories were deliberately run down by bishops who were more concerned with reforms and learning, for which new buildings were needed. Jesus College, Cambridge, was once a nunnery, while St John's College, Cambridge, was augmented by the suppression of two small nunneries. Cardinal Wolsey's plans to found colleges at Oxford and Ipswich resulted in the suppression of twenty-nine houses of monks, canons or nuns between 1524 and 1529. Among these were Bayham, Daventry and St Frideswide's at Oxford, whose site became that of Cardinal College, and whose church is now the college chapel and cathedral of Christ Church, Oxford.

By about 1530 there were about eight hundred English monasteries and nunneries still existing fairly successfully, still well populated and with their services devoutly carried out. This was about two hundred fewer than at their thirteenth-century peak. They may be broken down by orders as follows:

	monasteries	nunneries
Augustinian	170	23
Benedictine	282	92
Bonshommes	2	
Carthusian	9	
Cistercian	80	29
Cluniac	32	
Gilbertine	14	+10 double
Grandmontine	3	
Premonstratensian	34	4

Many buildings had been rebuilt but a lot of monasteries had by now fallen below their former high ideals, and the conduct of some monastic officials could justly be criticised and in a few cases was quite infamous.

A report on the state and conditions and finances of the monasteries was made by Royal Commissioners for Henry VIII and his chief minister, Thomas Cromwell. There is no doubt that the Commissioners often took care to discover what the king wanted them to about monastic faults and weaknesses. Reforms may have been necessary to the monastic system, but instead of this there was virtual revolution. The *Valor Ecclesiasticus* gave the king the fullest details of the endowed values of monastic lands and properties, together with their revenues. He acted on it, and the first basis for the suppression of the monasteries was an Act of Parliament of 1536 by which the smaller religious houses – those with a net annual income of under £200 – were to be dissolved, the property and income going to the Crown, and the inmates transferred to larger houses or pensioned off.

Waltham Abbey, Essex, was the last of the abbeys to surrender to Henry VIII.

It was in the north of England that monasteries so dissolved were most missed. Poor people who had benefited from their charities suffered, especially after bad harvests, and they wanted the monasteries back. They set out for London on the Pilgrimage of Grace, hoping to see the king and ask for the removal of his hated adviser, Cromwell. Some monasteries, with their abbots, became involved, but the rising was met by the king's representative long before it reached London. He promised the rebels a free pardon and invited their leader to London, but by then it seemed likely to the rebels that nothing would come of their efforts, so they went home. Many were subsequently executed.

This threat prompted the king to further action against the remaining monasteries, and the Suppression Act of 1539 brought the Dissolution of the Monasteries into its final stages. The last to go were the biggest foundations, culminating in 1540 with the surrender of Waltham Abbey. By then some 5000 monks, 2000 canons regular and 2000 nuns had been pensioned off. Others had been appointed to various benefices. A few who had openly resisted the Suppression Acts were executed, and the monastic buildings and estates passed into the king's hands, later to be sold to rich laymen.

Cathedral-priories served by Benedictine monks became secular collegiate cathedrals, with the prior replaced by a dean and the monks by a chapter of canons. Thus Canterbury, Carlisle, Durham, Ely, Norwich, Rochester, Winchester and Worcester were revived, and existing monastic buildings adapted to the new needs of secular clergy. Six other monastic churches became the basis for new bishoprics, at Bristol, Chester, Gloucester, Oxford, Peterborough and, temporarily, Westminster, which achieved cathedral status, although it was subsequently reduced to a collegiate church.

Numerically more important was the total or partial preservation of many monastic churches. In a number of these the nave had already been used as a parish church, and the Dissolution did allow for parishioners to retain the nave for their own continued use, while the choir and transepts would be left to decay and collapse or were deliberately destroyed. At Malmesbury, Chepstow, Binham, Waltham, Leominster, Wymondham, Blyth, Shrewsbury, Thorney, Lanercost, Dunstable and Worksop the nave is in use as the parish church; at Crowland it is the north aisle which now serves as the church; at Pershore the parishioners exchanged the nave for the much finer chancel; at Cartmel only the south chancel aisle was used as the parish church, and it is still known as the Town Choir. At Bolton Priory the nave is now the parish church; the chancel is in ruins. Christchurch Priory and Selby Abbey have survived in their entirety more by accident than by the intention of the parishioners. By contrast, Tewkesbury Abbey survives complete as a church because the parishioners were not satisfied with only the nave and they raised the £453 needed to buy the whole structure. Dorchester Abbey church is complete because one man, Richard Bewfforest, was generous enough to buy it – for £140 – and bequeath it to the parishioners. Abbey Dore, in Herefordshire, has the distinction of being the only English example of a Cistercian abbey church whose presbytery and chancel are in parochial use.

Lanercost Priory in Cumbria, where the church was partly taken into parochial use.

Dunstable Priory, Bedfordshire: much of the nave survives as St Peter's church.

Many monasteries eventually passed into the hands of laymen and were wholly or partly demolished for the building materials they offered. Some were converted into fine country houses or large farms: Cleeve, Lacock, Muchelney, Forde, Coverham, Wenlock, Woodspring, Milton Abbas, Stoneleigh. It is usually the claustral buildings that were turned into houses, but at Woodspring the monastery church became the basis for the farmhouse.

There was no Dissolution in Scotland, as it was still an independent nation over which Henry VIII's jurisdiction and power did not apply. Thus there was no single date at which Scottish monasteries ceased to exist, although the wave of new religious thought and ideas culminating in the Scottish Reformation of around 1560 brought about a slow end to monastic life. Lay commendators or even lay abbots assumed control of individual properties without necessarily driving out the monks. Many buildings remained in a reasonable state of repair, but gradually monastic life died out, a generation after it had ceased in the abbeys of England and Wales.

Principal monastic sites in England

✣ ✣ ✣ ✣ ✣ ✣

Please note that opening times may change and intending visitors should check ahead before making a long journey.

Bedfordshire

BUSHMEAD PRIORY   Augustinian
On an unclassified road near Colmworth, 2 miles east of B660. English Heritage. Open July and August, Saturdays, Sundays and bank holidays.

The priory was founded in 1185. What survives is the thirteenth-century frater, which formed the south claustral range with kitchen adjoining. It was divided horizontally after the Dissolution. It retains the original timber-framed roof and has good stained glass in sixteenth-century windows and interesting wall-paintings. There is nothing else monastic.

DUNSTABLE PRIORY   Augustinian
In the town centre. Nave in parochial use.

Little remains of the buildings of the priory founded in 1131, except the outer gatehouse. A substantial part of the nave survives as St Peter's parish church, late twelfth-century, with a magnificent north-west portal, rebuilt about 1240–50, and the fifteenth-century north-west tower.

ELSTOW ABBEY   Benedictine
1 mile south of Bedford, off A6.

Part of the nave of a nunnery founded in 1075 survives as the parish church. To its north is a large detached fifteenth-century bell-tower, but the so-called chapter-house south of the west front was the outer parlour of claustral buildings, with unique thirteenth-century vaulting. The remainder of the west range of the cloister is hidden in the early seventeenth-century Hillersden Hall.

Elstow Abbey, Bedfordshire: the bell-tower and the nave, now the parish church.

Berkshire

HURLEY PRIORY   Benedictine
By the south bank of the river Thames, 3¹/₂ miles east of Henley. Nave of church in parochial use.

The priory was founded in 1086. The long narrow nave of the priory church survives with mainly Norman windows and doorways, and the frater range to the north is incorporated into a private house. A probable monastic circular dovecote and a nearby large barn, both to the west of the church, date from the early fourteenth century.

READING ABBEY   Benedictine
Between Shire Hall and the prison. Fragmented ruins.

Founded for Cluniac monks in 1121 by Henry I, who was subsequently buried there, Reading became the only Cluniac house to be granted abbey status. It became Benedictine in the thirteenth century. Disparate cliffs of flint or rubble walling survive near a car park for local offices, but a tall roofless shell of the chapter-house gives a melancholy hint of former grandeur. The thirteenth-century gatehouse, restored in 1869, survives intact and is used as a museum.

Buckinghamshire

BRADWELL PRIORY   Benedictine
In Milton Keynes, about 1¹/₂ miles south of Wolverton, south of A422. Privately owned.

Founded in 1136, Bradwell Priory seems to have been a small and poor house throughout its existence, with only three monks in 1431. Outbuildings of Abbey Farm, west of the parish church, include fragments from the fourteenth-century monastic church. Excavations revealed a monastic bakehouse.

NOTLEY ABBEY   Augustinian
7 miles south-west of Aylesbury, north of A418. Now a private house not open to the public, but there is a good view of it from the road, and nearby public footpath.

Notley Abbey was founded about 1160 on a site by the river Thame. The west claustral range and the early sixteenth-century abbot's house survive, incorporated into a later mansion. The church has largely vanished, but on the hill to the west is the prominent square monastic dovecote, probably of the fourteenth century.

Cambridgeshire

DENNY ABBEY   Benedictine
6 miles north of Cambridge on A10. English Heritage. Open daily, April to October, afternoons.

Denny Abbey was founded in 1159 for Benedictine monks. From 1170 to 1312 it was used by Knights Templars and from 1342 to 1539 by Franciscan nuns.

What appears to be a Georgian farmhouse is the outer shell enclosing remains of part of a Norman monastic church, and showing evidence of the three successive religious groups who occupied and adapted it to their uses. Originally founded as a place of retreat for monks from Ely, it was soon acquired by the Knights Templars, whose order was abolished in 1312. Thirty years later the nuns of St Clare moved to Denny from their house at Waterbeach, and at the same time the nave, crossing and transepts of the monks' church were con-

Denny Abbey, Cambridgeshire: the site now houses the Farmland Museum of agricultural history.

verted into domestic use by the Countess of Pembroke. All the Norman crossing arches are clearly seen inside the building, with fourteenth-century doorways inserted.

To the north of the site of the cloister, the fourteenth-century refectory is well preserved, later converted to a barn. Excavations have revealed that there was a raised dais at its eastern end for the abbess, with the central floor area tiled throughout. A painting (1993) by Terry Ball depicts Poor Clare nuns in the refectory.

ELY CATHEDRAL-PRIORY
Benedictine
In Ely. In use as a cathedral.

Founded in 673 by Etheldreda for nuns and monks, Ely was destroyed in 870 and refounded in 970 as an abbey for monks. Rebuilding started in 1083, creating the nucleus of the present structure. In 1109 the monastic estates were divided, with the bishop in charge of the new diocese and the prior of the monastic community.

The nave, completed in 1189, is mainly early Norman, high, long and narrow, with alternating round and square pillars. The original chancel was extended during the second quarter of the thirteenth century, but the Norman crossing-tower collapsed in 1322. It was rebuilt almost immediately in stone, in the unique octagonal form we see today. Twenty years later it was crowned by the timber lantern largely renewed in the nineteenth century. Contemporary with the tower is the lovely spacious Lady Chapel with its unique lierne star-vault.

Most of the cloister buildings have vanished, except for two doorways, but other monastic buildings survive. Incorporated into more recent structures are the guest-house and the prior's lodging with a fine undercroft. Nearby is Prior Crauden's Chapel (1324) with splendid floor tiles. The Ely Porta, the great south gatehouse to the precinct, was begun in 1397.

On the eastern side of the precinct is the huge monastic infirmary, with nave and aisles, together with its ancillary buildings and the cellarer's range. Many precinct buildings with their undercrofts are happily preserved through being used either for diocesan administration or by King's School, founded by Henry VIII.

ISLEHAM PRIORY
Benedictine
In Isleham village, 16 miles north-east of Cambridge, on B1104. English Heritage. Freely open at any reasonable time. Keyholder's address given on site.

Founded in the late eleventh century, the priory's early Norman chapel of

Peterborough Cathedral: the west front of the abbey church.

nave, chancel and apse, with herringbone masonry and small windows, represents the unaltered shell, the first stage of a monastic church.

PETERBOROUGH ABBEY
Benedictine

In city centre. In use as diocesan cathedral.

The abbey was first founded in 656 and refounded in 966. The present building replaced one destroyed by fire and was begun in 1116, continuing well into the thirteenth century. The abbey was raised to cathedral status two years after the Dissolution and the Norman church survives almost complete. Most of the nave was completed by 1175, and the unusually powerful west front about sixty years later. The beautiful retro-choir replaced some Norman apses and represents the last work on the monastic church.

Monastic buildings were to the south, where the cloister area is now an open courtyard. To its south-east are impressive remains of the mid-thirteenth-century infirmary, whose seven-bay nave has delicate arches and good blank arcading. The former guest-house is now the deanery and the abbot's house is largely the Victorianised bishop's palace, above medieval undercrofts.

Splendid gateways survive, retaining medieval details with Victorian additions. The outer gate was remodelled in 1300; the abbot's gate is slightly earlier, the richly decorated priory gateway early sixteenth-century.

RAMSEY ABBEY
Benedictine

10 miles south-east of Peterborough, on the south-east edge of Ramsey. National Trust. Open March to October, daily.

Founded in 969, Ramsey became one of the wealthiest houses in England. There are no monastic remains, as an early seventeenth-century mansion covers the site. Part of the ornate gatehouse of 1500 is now preserved by the National Trust, its opulence illustrating the prestige of the great abbey which lay beyond.

THORNEY ABBEY
Benedictine

7 miles north-east of Peterborough, by B1040, just south of A47. Church in parochial use.

Everything of the monastery, founded in 972, has gone except for seven bays of the nave of the Norman church built between 1085 and 1108. The nave was restored about 1638, following the draining of the fens by the then Earl of Bedford, and the present transepts were added in 1830.

Cheshire

BIRKENHEAD PRIORY
Benedictine

In Priory Road, Birkenhead.

Only fragments survive of the priory founded about 1150. The well-preserved Norman chapter-house is used as a chapel, and there are remains of the north and west claustral ranges, including the frater undercroft and the wall of the guest-house and prior's lodging.

CHESTER CATHEDRAL
Benedictine

Near the centre of Chester, off Eastgate Street. In use as a diocesan cathedral.

Founded in 1093, the abbey church became a cathedral in 1541, its last abbot becoming dean. The church is complete, but with little Norman work remaining. There is much nineteenth-century restoration, but very fine fourteenth-century choir-stalls and misericords survive.

Claustral buildings are unusually complete and include the refectory with its pulpit, the thirteenth-century chapter-house and vestibule, cloister walks with lavatorium and carrels, and the Norman undercroft of the west range. West of the cloisters is Abbey Square, formerly part of the monastic precinct, with the fourteenth-century gatehouse in its south-western corner.

NORTON PRIORY
Augustinian

By minor road off A558, at the north-eastern edge of Runcorn, in a parkland setting. Norton Priory Museum Trust. Open daily from noon.

Norton Priory was founded in 1134. In 1971–83 it was excavated for public display, showing the layout of church, chapter-house, dormitory and cloisters, and how these were extended and developed to meet the needs of a growing community. The west range has a fine arcaded passage, a later twelfth-century undercroft and a richly carved Norman doorway.

Cornwall

ST GERMANS PRIORY
Augustinian

In St Germans village, 4 miles west of Saltash, on B3249. In use as parish church.

Although founded in 1180, the priory was not consecrated until 1261. There are no claustral remains, but the conventual church survives almost complete, apart from its chancel, which collapsed in 1592. Its situation is memorable. Its west front, with twin towers, shows in its portal Cornwall's best Norman architecture.

Cumbria

CALDER ABBEY
Cistercian

4 miles south-east of Egremont off A595 at Calder Bridge. Privately owned. Viewable from footpath.

Colonised by monks from Furness in 1135, Calder became Cistercian in

Calder Abbey, Cumbria.

1147. Poorly endowed and suffering from repeated Scottish raids, it never flourished. Considerable ruins of the church survive, and part of the east claustral range. The south range is incorporated into an eighteenth-century house.

CARLISLE CATHEDRAL
Augustinian
In the city centre. In use as a diocesan cathedral.

Founded in 1133, the priory was immediately elevated to cathedral status, retained at the Dissolution. Its eight-bay nave and two-bay chancel were changed in the fourteenth century to an eight-bay chancel, and in the Civil War with a two-bay nave. As the chancel is 12 feet (3.7 metres) wider than the nave, everything looks wrong! There is a magnificent east window, fine sculpture, fifteenth-century choir-stalls, canopies and misericords.

Of monastic buildings, the frater is almost completely preserved, now used as the chapter-house and cathedral library. Prior Slee's gatehouse of 1527 is now the main entrance to the cathedral precinct.

CARTMEL PRIORY
Augustinian
6 miles east of Ulverston, reached by minor roads off B5277. Church in parochial use.

Cartmel Priory was founded in 1188. The church was spared at the Dissolution and extensively restored in 1618. It is famous for the low square lantern set

Cartmel Priory: the fourteenth-century gatehouse leading to the Market Place.

✣ 49 ✣

Furness Abbey, Cumbria: impressive ruins showing the thirteenth-century arches of the cloisters.

diagonally on the crossing-tower. Lively misericords enrich fifteenth-century stalls. In the Market Place, the neat simple fourteenth-century monastic gatehouse survives.

FURNESS ABBEY   Cistercian
6 miles north of Barrow-in-Furness on minor road off A590. English Heritage. Open daily throughout the year.

Founded in 1127 by Savignac monks and absorbed into the Cistercian order in 1147, Furness became the second wealthiest Cistercian house in England. Extensive ruins in local red sandstone follow the usual Cistercian plan, although restrictions of the site prevented elaboration of the west front of the church.

Church transepts and the choir and the west belfry tower stand almost to their original height. The fifteenth-century presbytery contains sumptuous sedilia and piscina, but the eastern range of the cloister, Furness's great glory, has five arches framing book cupboards, parlour, slype and the arcade of the chapter-house. Good examples of monastic control of water exist throughout the site, to the east of which are ruins of the abbot's house. To the west are the tall ruins of the infirmary hall and chapel, with foundations of the octagonal kitchen built in the late thirteenth century. North-west of the precinct are reconstructed parts of the outer gatehouse with its adjoining *capella extra portas*.

HOLME CULTRAM ABBEY   Cistercian
At Abbey Town, 15 miles west of Carlisle, on B5307. Church in parochial use.

The abbey was founded in 1150. Six of the nine bays of the nave of the Cistercian church survive, shorn of their aisles, as St Mary's parish church. The twelfth-century work includes a glorious west portal, but much is Georgian. There are no monastic remains.

LANERCOST PRIORY   Augustinian
2 miles north-east of Brampton by minor road off A69. English Heritage. Open daily, 1st April to 31st October.

Founded in 1166, Lanercost suffered during Scottish wars of the late thirteenth and fourteenth centuries.

Shap Abbey, Cumbria: the west tower.

The church was allowed to stand empty for two centuries after the Dissolution. The east end was sealed, the church restored and reroofed about 1740 to serve as the parish church (not English Heritage). The roofless crossing and chancel are now a noble ruin with a sturdy tower.

The layout of claustral buildings south of the church includes the well-preserved undercroft of the frater in the south range. The west range was converted into a dwelling house after the Dissolution, and at its southern end is a typical north-country pele-tower, which was the prior's house. Further west, at the precinct entrance, is an inner arch of the gateway.

SHAP ABBEY   Premonstratensian
1¹/₂ miles west of Shap, off M6 (junction 39) and A6. English Heritage. Freely open at all reasonable times.

Shap Abbey was founded in 1201 on a remote, beautiful but cramped site by the river Lowther. Little survives except the imposing early-sixteenth-century west tower of the church.

Devon

BUCKLAND ABBEY   Cistercian
6 miles south of Tavistock, off A386 south of Yelverton. National Trust. Open daily, April to October, except Thursdays; November to March, Saturday and Sunday afternoons.

Founded in 1278, this was the last of the seventy-six Cistercian abbeys to be built in England and Wales. After the Dissolution most of the abbey church was remodelled as a house, subdivided horizontally to provide comfortable living accommodation, with more structural changes around 1800. Since 1951 it has been used by the City of Plymouth to display collections of items associated with the Grenville and Drake families, who lived there.

The church has lost its transepts but much of the remainder of the thirteenth-century structure, with its low central tower, survives. There is a presbytery, a short nave and a later chapel. Most of the claustral buildings have gone, but the

Buckland Abbey, Devon: the Great Barn.

precinct is dominated by the fifteenth-century Great Barn. Nearby, now used as the National Trust's shop and restaurant, is a contemporary structure probably intended as a stable, later converted to domestic use, possibly as a house for the reeve, or farm manager.

FRITHELSTOCK PRIORY   Augustinian
6 miles south of Bideford, on minor road between A386 and A388. Freely open.
   The only remains of the priory founded in 1229 are of the church, with tall west front and north wall with good lancets. The foundations and a blocked arch survive of the tower to the south. Cloisters were to the north, and nearby Church Farm occupies the site of the former prior's house.

TAVISTOCK ABBEY   Benedictine
In the centre of Tavistock. Fragmented remains can be easily seen.
   Most of the site of the abbey founded in 975 is now obscured by roads and

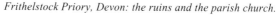

Frithelstock Priory, Devon: the ruins and the parish church.

Torre Abbey, Devon: the gatehouse leads to the forecourt of the house, now a museum and gallery.

modern buildings. The Court Gatehouse has a late twelfth-century core, and the Bedford Hotel occupies the site of the abbey frater. On the edge of the nearby parish churchyard are a few relics of the cloister, and a length of precinct wall survives alongside the River Walk. The former infirmary or abbot's lodging is now a Christian Brethren chapel.

TORRE ABBEY
Premonstratensian
In Abbey Gardens, Torquay, near the sea-front. Owned by Torbay Council. Open daily, April to October.
Torre Abbey was founded in 1196, but after the Dissolution much was left to collapse, although the south and west ranges of the claustral buildings were converted into a house about 1600, enlarged and altered in following centuries. There is a two-arched gatehouse, the medieval abbot's tower and an archway to the ruined chapter-house. The frater was transformed in Georgian times, but there is a thirteenth-century barn with a gabled central doorway.

Dorset

ABBOTSBURY ABBEY
Benedictine
In Abbotsbury, off B3157, near the churchyard. English Heritage. Free entry at all reasonable times.
The abbey was founded in 1026 for secular canons, replaced by monks in 1044. Meagre remains include the north wall of the monastic church in the parish churchyard, the ruined gable-end of a claustral building, a dovecote and the superb barn, *c.*1400, of which half is roofed and thatched. There are remains of two gatehouses, one incorporated into a private house.

CERNE ABBAS
Benedictine
North of Cerne Abbas village. Parts incorporated into a private house.
The ruins of the abbey, founded in 987, have not been excavated, because the parish churchyard occupies the site of the monastic church. Parts of three monastic buildings survive: the porch to the abbot's hall, with a fan-vaulted arch and two-storeyed oriel; the simpler, two-storey guest-house, also fifteenth-century; and a small barn to its north-west.

CHRISTCHURCH PRIORY
Augustinian
In Christchurch town, south of the centre. In parochial use.
Only the church of the priory founded in 1094 survives, as one of England's longest parish churches, particularly well seen from the north. There is much outstanding Norman work, and a four-bay chancel, early sixteenth-century, as it was when the canons finally left. Two doorways in the nave south aisle led to the cloister, but no claustral buildings remain.

Christchurch Priory, Dorset: arcading on the exterior of the north transept.

FORDE ABBEY
Cistercian

Near the Somerset border, 4 miles south-east of Chard. Now a house. Open April to October, Sundays, Tuesdays to Fridays.

Forde Abbey was founded in 1141. The church has gone but what remains is a memorable display of claustral buildings incorporated into a mansion in the mid seventeenth century, and occupied, little altered, since then. The thirteenth-century upper-floor dormitory, with its undercroft, is fully preserved, as is much of the fifteenth-century frater. The Norman chapter-house is now a private chapel. The last abbot, Thomas Chard, 1521–39, built himself princely new apartments, including a great hall and ostentatious porch, and began to remodel the cloisters. His work forms an important part of Edmund Prideaux's later mansion.

MILTON ABBEY
Benedictine

At Milton Abbas, 6 miles south-west of Blandford. Largely incorporated into an eighteenth-century mansion, now a school (not open to the public), the church becoming its chapel (frequently open).

Founded in 964, the monastery was destroyed by fire in 1309, but the church was not fully rebuilt. Only the choir, crossing and transepts survive. Their fourteenth-century elegance and fine proportions are rather cold and bare, following a ruthless internal stripping in the 1750s.

SHERBORNE ABBEY
Benedictine

Church in parochial use. Some monastic buildings are now used as part of a public school.

Sherborne was a bishopric from 705 to 1075; the house became an abbey in 1122. Stephen Harding, who later drew up the constitution of the Cistercian order, was then a novice at Sherborne. Much of the Norman church was destroyed by fire in 1437 following a riot between the monks and parishioners. Its beautiful, mainly Perpendicular successor has fine fan-vaulting in the presbytery and nave. The crossing arches and some transept walling survive from the Norman building, together with the south porch. The cloisters lay to the north, where parts of the monks' dormitory, the abbot's hall and kitchen are incorporated into school buildings, while to the east, at the town centre, is the early sixteenth-century hexagonal conduit or lavatorium, formerly within the cloister.

Durham

DURHAM CATHEDRAL-PRIORY   Benedictine
At the medieval heart of Durham city. Cathedral in episcopal use.

The priory was founded in 1083, but the foundation stone was laid ten years later. It is the major British example of early Norman architecture, and probably the most famous monastic house in Britain.

The great church was completed in forty years, the only subsequent additions being the Galilee Chapel of 1175, and the replacement of the eastern end by the Chapel of the Nine Altars in the thirteenth century.

Monastic buildings around the cloister are excellently preserved. The cloister arcades were rebuilt in the late fourteenth and early fifteenth centuries. Chapter-house, parlour and slype remain very much as originally built, while the modern Deanery, the monks' dormitory of the 1070s, incorporates, together with the undercroft of the south range, the oldest work at Durham. Remodelled in 1476, it was used as the prior's lodging.

The present cathedral library on the first floor of the south range was formerly the frater, with the kitchen to its south, now the muniment room. The first floor of the west claustral range, originally a dormitory, now houses the cathedral museum, which displays manuscripts and other items, including the coffin of St Cuthbert, in whose honour the cathedral-priory was built. In a fascinating book, *The Rites of Durham*, written in 1593 by a man who was a monk at Durham in his youth, we read that at the Dissolution forty monks were there. A few months after it surrendered in December 1540 the priory was reconstituted as a cathedral with a dean and twelve prebendaries.

EGGLESTONE ABBEY   Premonstratensian
1¹/₂ miles south-east of Barnard Castle, by a minor road. English Heritage. Free access at any reasonable time.

Founded between 1195 and 1198, Egglestone Abbey is beautifully situated above the Tees. It remained a poor abbey throughout its history. Of its church, the walls of the nave and presbytery stand to considerable height, with the west wall of the south transept. Little survives of the claustral buildings apart from some mutilated walls of the east range, much of which was converted into a house after the Dissolution. At the end of the east range is the undercroft of the reredorter, with a very impressive drain running along its north wall.

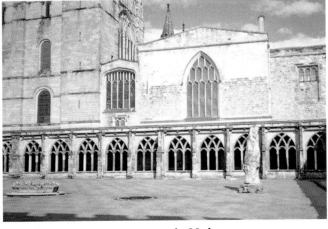

Durham Cathedral: the cloisters of the former priory.

Finchale Priory, Durham.

FINCHALE PRIORY   Benedictine
3 miles north-east of Durham on minor road off A167. English Heritage. Open daily, April to September.

This was founded on a riverside site where two monks from Durham had occupied an earlier hermitage until about 1196, when it became a priory for eight monks. Substantial remains of the church survive, with long transepts, presbytery, and nave complete to the eaves. The frater walls stand equally high, with a vaulted undercroft. South of the chancel, and projecting beyond its eastern end, is the prior's house with its undercroft.

From the fourteenth century Finchale Priory became a rest house for monks from Durham, groups of four coming every three weeks, to stay with the permanent staff of a prior and four monks, and dining at the prior's table. The original frater and other claustral buildings became redundant.

JARROW PRIORY   Benedictine
In Jarrow, on minor road north of A185 and 1 mile south-east of the southern entrance to the Tyne road tunnel. Chancel of St Paul's monastic church in parochial use. Monastic ruins, English Heritage. Freely open at all reasonable times.

The first foundation in 681 was by Benedict Biscop, a Northumbrian nobleman who also founded nearby Wearmouth. The two monasteries became a centre of learning, where the great scholar Bede spent all his working life, entering Wearmouth as a child of seven in 680, moving to Jarrow a few years later, and remaining there until his death in 735, apart from occasional journeys to York and Lindisfarne.

The seventh-century monastic church which Bede knew is the chancel of the present church. On the east wall of the nave, above the chancel arch, is the oldest surviving dedication stone in Britain, its Latin inscription giving the date 23rd April 685. Three small windows in the south wall of the chancel, and the lower stages of the tower, are also of the early monastic church, the rest of the tower dating from *c.*1080. The present nave was rebuilt in 1783 and again a century later.

St Bololph's Priory, Colchester: the west front of the Norman church.

No early monastic buildings survive above ground, but of the post-Conquest refoundation some fragments stand, including the east wall of the west range and the north wall of the south range.

Essex

COLCHESTER: ST BOTOLPH'S PRIORY   Augustinian canons
Near Colchester Town station. English Heritage. Free access at all reasonable times.
St Botolph's was the first Augustinian priory in England, founded about 1095. Considerable ruins of its early Norman church survive, showing mighty circular piers of flint, septaria and Roman brick, with a gallery above, all rather grim. The broad west front has two tiers of intersected arches, but nothing survives of the twin towers, nor of the transepts and eastern end of the church. All claustral buildings have gone.

COLCHESTER: ST JOHN'S ABBEY GATE   Benedictine
South of town centre. English Heritage. Exterior freely visible.
Only this fifteenth-century gatehouse survives of the abbey. The outer façade is flint with ornate flushwork, but the inner face is much plainer. Flanking polygonal corner turrets have pinnacles with battlements between.

LITTLE COGGESHALL   Cistercian
South of Coggeshall village, off A120, 9 miles west of Colchester, down a rough farm track opposite Grange Barn. Grange Barn (National Trust): open April to mid October, Tuesday, Thursday, Sunday and bank holiday afternoons.
The *capella ante portas* survives, as the chapel of St Nicholas, a plain rectangular building, kept locked. Dating from 1225, its brick dressings are regarded as the earliest medieval brickwork (not re-used Roman) in England.
Grange Barn belonged to the Cistercian abbey, dates from 1140 and is the oldest surviving timber-framed barn in Europe.

Prittlewell Priory, Essex, is now a museum owned by Southend-on-Sea Council.

LITTLE DUNMOW PRIORY
Augustinian canons

6 miles west of Braintree, south of A120. South chancel chapel of priory church now used as the parish church. Locked, but key available at nearby house.

The long narrow building, unbalanced in appearance, is architecturally fascinating, its north wall being the chancel south arcade of what was a huge priory church. Opposite five bays of thick piers are, on the south, the magnificently opulent windows of a 1360 remodelling, with blank arcades, sculptured leaves and animals. Two alabaster effigies on a tomb-chest are of remarkably high quality, and very dignified.

PRITTLEWELL PRIORY
Cluniac

In the northern part of Southend, in a public park. Belongs to Southend-on-Sea Council. Open daily except Monday.

Founded in 1110 and enlarged twice, the priory subsequently declined. The church was demolished at the Dissolution and most of the claustral parts have gone. The fifteenth-century frater, much restored, is now a museum. The west range contained the prior's lodging.

ST OSYTH'S PRIORY
Augustinian canons

10 miles south-east of Colchester, off B1027. Privately owned.

Founded about 1161 on the site of a Saxon nunnery, St Osyth's Priory was incorporated into a mansion after the Dissolution. The church has vanished, but thirteenth-century undercrofts survive of the east and west claustral ranges, and the thirteenth-century frater lobby. The splendidly ostentatious gatehouse was built about 1475 and shows the highest quality of East Anglian flushwork.

TILTY ABBEY
Cistercian

7¹/₂ miles north-east of Bishop's Stortford, reached along minor roads and narrow lanes. Church in parochial use.

This beautiful, very rare survival justifies a detour, being formerly the *capella ante portas* of the abbey founded in 1153. The Early English nave had added to it in the early fourteenth century a larger, sumptuous chancel with a handsome east window. Fragments of medieval walls are in the fields north of the church.

WALTHAM ABBEY — Augustinian canons

In Waltham Abbey, off A112. Nave, with Lady Chapel, in use as parish church.

The Norman seven-bay nave, the fourteenth-century Lady Chapel and a west wall of similar date are the surviving fragments of one of the greatest medieval abbeys. Architectural details are similar to, though less grand than Durham. The west tower, added in 1556–8, signified the change from monastic to parochial use.

North of the church's west front is the splendid fourteenth-century gatehouse (English Heritage).

Gloucestershire

BRISTOL ABBEY — Augustinian

In city centre. Church in use as a diocesan cathedral.

Founded in 1140, dissolved in 1539 but reconstituted by Henry VIII in 1542, Bristol never became a large monastery, with twenty or fewer canons during its last 150 years. The church dates mainly from the first third of the fourteenth century, with an architecturally unusual chancel-nave in the form of a broad, relatively low hall with aisles the same height as the nave. Four chapels project from it, and a new nave was added between 1868 and 1888 to replace the Norman one destroyed at the Dissolution.

Of the claustral buildings, the late twelfth-century chapter-house is the main survival, little altered apart from a rebuilt east wall. To its south are the slype and dorter undercroft. The frater in the south range now houses the cathedral school, and the great gateway to the west of the nave, built about 1200, had its upper parts rebuilt at the end of the fifteenth century.

DEERHURST — Benedictine

3 miles south-west of Tewkesbury, at end of minor road west of A38. Church in parochial use.

Deerhurst is the best surviving example of a Saxon monastic church. Mentioned in 804, it was rebuilt in the late tenth century, but Deerhurst ceased to be an abbey before the Conquest, since when many changes of plan and ownership have occurred.

The nave is probably on the original plan and was raised to its present height about 975. Two pairs of two-storey porticoes extending north and south are probably of the early church, and the existing west porch was

Deerhurst, Gloucestershire, is the best surviving example of a Saxon monastic church.

raised to tower height at the tenth-century restoration.

The arrangements of many Saxon doorways and windows can be explained only by the complicated building history. There is eighth- and tenth-century sculpture and a ninth-century font.

FLAXLEY ABBEY   Cistercian
In the Forest of Dean, by minor road off A48, 2¹/₂ miles north-east of Cinderford. Ruins incorporated into a private house, not open to the public, but easily seen from the parish churchyard.

Founded in 1151, never becoming large or wealthy, Flaxley Abbey served as a royal hunting lodge; the lay brothers' frater was a guest hall and the abbot's guest chamber was used exclusively by Edward III.

The church had been destroyed by fire before the Dissolution, and from the seventeenth century the south and west claustral ranges were adapted for domestic use. On the west is a seventeenth-century façade above a rib-vaulted undercroft, and to the south is a late Georgian front with later Gothick windows. In the angle between the two the abbot's hall can be identified by its fourteenth-century window.

GLOUCESTER CATHEDRAL-PRIORY   Benedictine
Near the centre of Gloucester. In episcopal use as a cathedral.

Gloucester Priory was founded in 1058 and after the Dissolution its church was retained for cathedral use. Gloucester was one of the most important English Benedictine houses but an extensive building programme in the thirteenth century caused financial problems. Help from the Crown and the burial in Gloucester in 1327 of the murdered Edward II made the monastery a place of pilgrimage. Offerings helped to finance a rebuilding programme which has given us much of the present superb church.

Norman work survives in the crypt, ambulatory and its radiating chapels, and the massive circular piers of the seven eastern bays of the nave, with small triforium above. The north and south transepts had a veneer of Perpendicular panelling added between 1331 and 1373, but it is the chancel – the choir and presbytery of the monastic church – restructured from 1337, which represents the beginning of the unique English Gothic now called Perpendicular, with its distinctive use of soaring, straight-line verticals, together with horizontal transoms. The great central tower, built in the middle of the fifteenth century, is 225 feet (69 metres) high, patterned with successive tiers of blank arcading, crowned with an open coronet and pinnacles.

The cloisters north of the church, built between 1375 and 1410, survive completely, innovatively fan-vaulted. On the south walk are twenty recessed carrels, while the western half of the north walk is the lavatorium, where monks washed their hands before meals. North of the north transept is the slype, used as a parlour, and the twelfth-century chapter-house, partly barrel-vaulted. A nearby staircase probably led to a library. Most of the other monastic buildings have gone.

HAILES ABBEY   Cistercian
2 miles north-east of Winchcombe, off B4632. National Trust and English Heritage. Open daily, April to October.

Founded by Richard, Earl of Cornwall, a son of King John, as late as 1246, Hailes Abbey was colonised from Beaulieu. In 1270 the founder's son presented to Hailes a phial of the Holy Blood, which subsequently brought many pilgrims and financial rewards, allowing the east end of the church to be rebuilt, to display the relic, in the unusual form of a chevet – an apse with ambulatory and radiating chapels. Of this, and the rest of the church, little survives but the

Hailes Abbey, Gloucestershire: the cloister arches.

foundations of the plan marked out on the mown grass. Elsewhere there are low walls of the cloisters, with some arches in the west range and, in the east, the entrance to the chapter-house, and a processional door to the south wall of the nave aisle.

Many sculptured fragments, including exceptionally fine carved bosses, are well displayed in a good museum by the entrance.

KINGSWOOD ABBEY Cistercian.
Gatehouse only. In Kingswood, off B4060, 1 mile south-west of Wotton-under-Edge. English Heritage. Freely visible at any time. Key for interior obtainable nearby.

Kingswood was founded in 1139 and colonised from Tintern. By 1276 it had become prosperous through its sales of wool. All the buildings have gone, except for a small section of precinct wall and the late fourteenth-century vaulted gatehouse, with pinnacled buttresses, finials, niches and delicate carving.

LEONARD STANLEY PRIORY Benedictine
In Leonard Stanley, 3¹/2 miles west of Stroud, south of A419. Church in parochial use.

Founded in 1121–9 originally for Augustinian canons, the priory was granted to the Benedictines of St Peter's, Gloucester, in 1146. Only the conventual church survives, mainly Norman, with a wide, aisleless parishioners' nave, massive central tower, chancel and transepts. Other priory buildings to the south are obscured among farmyard structures, where a large barn has a medieval gable end, a blocked doorway and a fourteenth-century window.

TEWKESBURY ABBEY
Benedictine
In Tewkesbury town centre. Church in parochial use.
The first Saxon foundation, dating from 715, was twice destroyed by Danes. A new church, started in 1102, was consecrated in 1123. At the Dissolution almost all the monastic buildings were destroyed, but the Tewkesbury townsfolk, rightly claiming the nave of the church as their own, bought the eastern or conventual part for £453, for parochial use. Thus virtually the whole of the monastic church survives, not only architecturally outstanding, but containing an historic group of medieval tombs and chantries.

The church is Romanesque, largely unaltered since its completion, apart from the vaulting of nave and aisles, done between 1300 and 1340. The Norman tower dates from 1140–50, as does the enormous, six-columned arch of the great west front. Hugh Despenser and his wife, Elizabeth, remodelled the chancel during the first third of the fourteenth century, giving it apsidal chapels and a superb lierne vault. Here, in the presbytery, are all the glorious tombs and chantries.

Nothing remains of the claustral buildings. West of the church, Abbey House of 1520 may have been the abbot's lodging or the monastic guest-house.

Hampshire

BEAULIEU ABBEY
Cistercian
7 miles south-east of Lyndhurst, 14 miles south of Southampton. Privately owned, but open throughout the year as part of Beaulieu Palace.
King John's foundation of 1204 was colonised from Citeaux, acquired property, had extensive estates and was shrewdly administered. Uniquely, some of its account book survives. Unfortunately none of the church does, although its foundations and layout show it to have had the largest area of any Cistercian church – 336 feet (102 metres) long and 186 feet (57 metres) wide across the transepts.

Monastic buildings were south of the church, and the cloister walls on the west survive, where the lay brothers' dormitory, much restored and roofed, contains a restaurant and the abbey museum. Between it and the cloister is the lay brothers' lane, giving access to the western bay of the church.

South of the cloister the monks' frater was converted at the Dissolution into the parish church. Extensively restored and added to, it retains the former monastic reader's pulpit, now serving as a normal pulpit. The unusual wagon roof dates from the fourteenth century.

Beaulieu Palace House developed from the great gatehouse and retains many medieval monastic features, especially the vaulting in the dining-room and inner hall, as well as wall arches and window tracery.

NETLEY ABBEY
Cistercian
In Netley, 4 miles south-east of Southampton, facing Southampton Water. English Heritage. Free access at all reasonable times.
Founded in 1239, Netley Abbey prospered for a century but then declined, suffering financially because too many mariners made demands on its hospitality and, possibly, because royal sailors from Southampton in 1338 stole its sheep and lambs.

The church was planned on a lavish scale with an aisled nave of eight bays and a four-bay chancel, two transepts and a low crossing-tower. The north transept has gone but many of the church's outer walls stand to triforium height. The west front and north nave wall show fourteenth-century tracery, and there are good processional doorways of the thirteenth century.

Netley Abbey, Hampshire: the nave and chancel.

Good claustral remains include the chapter-house, sacristy, warming-room, a parlour, the monks' reredorter block or infirmary and the abbot's lodging.

After the Dissolution the south claustral range was drastically altered to accommodate the gateway to a Tudor mansion, whose hall was the nave of the church with living-rooms built from the eastern range, and the cloister became a courtyard.

ROMSEY ABBEY   Benedictine nuns
In Romsey. In parochial use.

The abbey was first founded in 907 and Benedictine nuns were introduced sixty years later. Major rebuilding started about 1120 and continued for a century, giving us the finest church of any English nunnery, almost wholly intact, a masterpiece of Norman architecture, although the three western bays of the nave are Early English. There is a central crossing with a squat tower, transepts and side chapels.

Outside the west wall of the south transept is the famous Romsey Rood, a pre-Romanesque sculpture. No claustral buildings survive.

TITCHFIELD ABBEY   Premonstratensian
Half a mile north of Titchfield, off A27. English Heritage. Open at most reasonable times.

At the Dissolution the abbey was converted into a Tudor mansion, which was largely demolished in 1781. What remains is the shell of the spectacular gatehouse constructed from the nave of the abbey church, with four large turrets in the centre, and flanking wings. The best monastic survival is the ruined entrance to the chapter-house, subsequently incorporated into the Tudor façade of the east range of the former cloister. Some medieval tiles remain *in situ* in the cloister.

WINCHESTER CATHEDRAL-PRIORY   Benedictine
In Winchester. In use as an episcopal cathedral.

The priory was founded first in 643, secondly in 964, but rebuilding began in 1079, with alterations and additions continuing until the early sixteenth century. The church which survives is the longest in England, its oldest parts being the transepts and choir and a well-preserved crypt beneath the retro-choir. The twelve-bay nave was remodelled largely by Bishop Wykeham in the late fourteenth century. A late fifteenth- and early sixteenth-century great stone screen spans the chancel, and to its west are remarkable mortuary chests of Saxon kings and bishops.

Few claustral buildings survive, although a row of arches south of the south transept mark the entrances to the night-stairs, and there is good Norman arcading on the chapter-house arches.

The present Deanery was formerly the prior's lodging, and much of the precinct wall still stands.

Winchester Cathedral: Norman arcading of the former chapter-house.

Abbey Dore, Herefordshire, is the only Cistercian abbey church whose presbytery and chancel are in parochial use.

Herefordshire

ABBEY DORE   Cistercian

In the Golden Valley, 10 miles south-west of Hereford, by B4347 north of Ewyas Harold. Chancel, transepts and crossing of church in parochial use.

Founded in 1147, Abbey Dore was colonised from Morimond. Temporary buildings were replaced from about 1175. The nave of the church has gone, together with all monastic buildings which lay to the north. The transepts and vaulted aisled presbytery of three bays remain, with an ambulatory having a double walk at the eastern end, all with finely sculptured capitals. The preservation of the whole surviving eastern arm of the Cistercian church makes Abbey Dore unique in England and is the result of Lord Scudamore's restoration of 1633-4, when the little tower was added and the western parts were walled off. Timber ceilings, screen and stalls were the work of the local carpenter John Abel. The result is a remarkable and lovely building.

LEOMINSTER PRIORY   Benedictine
Initially for nuns, later for monks

At the eastern end of Church Street, east of the town centre. Church in parochial use.

The ninth-century nunnery was dissolved in 1046, manorial ownership being transferred to Reading Abbey in 1123, and the monks' building started soon after. Disputes with parishioners have resulted in the church having three naves, as well as a north aisle and a Norman west tower. The north aisle and nave are Norman (1150), the south (or middle) one from 1235, and the south aisle 1320. Transepts, chancel and a Lady Chapel have gone, like all the claustral buildings to the north except for the so-called Priory House, now in community use, and and which was probably the reredorter, infirmary and infirmary chapel.

St Albans Priory, Hertfordshire: the fourteenth-century gatehouse.

Hertfordshire

ST ALBANS CATHEDRAL-PRIORY   Benedictine
In the centre of the city. Since 1877 the seat of an episcopal see.

The priory was founded about 970 by St Oswald of Worcester and King Edgar. Rebuilding of the church began about 1077, with a nine-bay nave, a crossing with tower, a transept and an apsidal chancel. Three more bays were added by 1197, with a west front completed in 1230. Five nave piers collapsed in 1323, so much of the south side of the nave was rebuilt. This conflicts architecturally with the surviving northern Norman bays opposite, an unfortunate visual imbalance, not helped by an almost total lack of decorative detail.

Canterbury Cathedral: the cloisters.

St Augustine's Abbey, Canterbury, is the burial site of four Saxon kings.

The Norman monks used bricks and flints from the Roman *Verulamium*, which adds to the sombre impression. The present west front is an 1879 replacement of the medieval one. Of the vast claustral complex only the massive fourteenth-century gatehouse survives.

St Albans became wealthy and influential, especially in the thirteenth and fourteenth centuries. A St Albans monk, Matthew Paris, became one of the most famous chroniclers of medieval England. From his time until the Dissolution of 1539 the number of monks there remained at around fifty.

Kent

CANTERBURY CATHEDRAL-PRIORY   Benedictine
In the centre of Canterbury. In use as archiepiscopal cathedral.

This was initially a Saxon monastery, became a house of secular canons in the ninth century and was refounded as a Benedictine monastery in 997. Church and monastic buildings were rebuilt from 1070, but after Archbishop Becket's murder in 1170 and a serious fire four years later a new chancel was completed; in the fourteenth and fifteenth centuries the nave was rebuilt, with the central tower added in the early sixteenth century. Norman crypts survive beneath the whole of the eastern end.

Most of the Norman claustral buildings have been replaced by later ones in the same position, so the plan and huge scale can still be appreciated. The cloisters north of the church date from around 1400, as does the large rectangular chapter-house, detached from the north transept. To its north is the great Norman dorter, built to house up to 150 monks. The extensive infirmary buildings, hall and chapel are of the early twelfth century. The unique lavatory tower on the south walk of the infirmary cloister dates from 1150. Christ Church Gate, 1517–21, is the principal entrance from the town into the precinct.

CANTERBURY: ST AUGUSTINE'S ABBEY   Benedictine
In Longport, a quarter of a mile east of the cathedral close. English Heritage. Open all the year.

The abbey was founded in 598 by King Ethelbert and St Augustine. Between 613 and 827 three adjacent churches were built on the site, along a west-east alignment, and replaced in 1070 by a large new abbey church, but still leaving the easternmost St Pancras church isolated. Ruins reveal outlines of the seventh-century churches and the eleventh-century rotunda beneath Norman foundations. The great gateway dates from 1300–9.

MINSTER-IN-SHEPPEY PRIORY   Benedictine nuns
2 miles south-east of Sheerness, by B2008. Church in parochial use.
   Founded in 670 by St Sexburga, the priory was later deserted after Danish raids. It was refounded in 1087 but apparently became Augustinian in 1396. Part of the seventh-century nuns' church survives in the northern of two naves, to which were added a fourteenth-century chancel and a fifteenth-century tower. The thirteenth-century southern nave was for parochial use. The three-storey gatehouse was formerly used by the nuns' chaplain and the vicar of the parish church.

ROCHESTER CATHEDRAL-PRIORY   Benedictine
In Rochester town centre, off High Street. Parochial-conventual church in episcopal use.
   This was founded in 604, and again about 1080. The church is architecturally modest, essentially Romanesque of the mid twelfth century, with the chancel rebuilt in the early thirteenth century. The impressive west front is a remarkably well-balanced Norman composition with a large Perpendicular window.
   Of claustral buildings to the south, unusually joining the chancel rather than the nave, only the east range is readily recognised, the whole outer walk still standing with the early twelfth-century chapter-house and dorter undercroft. There was a two-bay vaulted lavatorium with a tower recess adjoining. North of the church is the fifteenth-century prior's gate.

ST RADEGUND'S ABBEY   Premonstratensian
3 miles west of Dover, off a minor road near Alkham and approached along a farm lane. Privately owned, but ruins quite visible.
   Founded in 1192 on what is still lonely chalk downland, the abbey's considerable ruins are largely incorporated into a farm and associated buildings. The remains of the monastic church tower, in the angle between the north transept and the aisleless nave, probably became a gatehouse in the sixteenth century. Cloisters to the south became the courtyard of a post-Dissolution house, which also included the chapter-house, frater and cellarer's buildings.

Lancashire

COCKERSAND PRIORY   Premonstratensian
By minor road 5 miles south-southwest of Lancaster. Privately owned.
   By the beach on the southern edge of the Lune estuary, only the thirteenth-century chapter-house of the priory founded in 1190 survives, long used as a mausoleum of the Dalton family. The fourteenth-century choir-stalls, luxuriantly canopied, now in St Mary's church, Lancaster, probably came from Cockersand.

SAWLEY (SALLEY) ABBEY   Cistercian
In Sawley village, off A59, 3¹/₂ miles north-east of Clitheroe. English Heritage. Freely open all year.
   Founded in 1147, Sawley Abbey never became either large or wealthy, suffering from Scottish raids, poor crops and harvests. Extensive though meagre ruins show lower courses of the church walls and some monastic buildings at the centre of well-preserved earthworks. The church was unusual in having a nave wider than its length, suggesting that it had been planned to be longer. The

Whalley Abbey, Lancashire: the fourteenth-century gatehouse.

chancel was widened in the sixteenth century by adding aisles. The south transept shows part of the night stairs. The most prominent claustral survival is the drain for the monks' reredorter.

WHALLEY ABBEY   Cistercian
In Whalley, 7 miles north-northeast of Blackburn, off A59 and A671. Owned by the Diocese of Blackburn, but open daily.

Whalley Abbey was founded in 1296. The monks had a succession of disputes, with nearby Sawley, with the Bishop of Coventry and Lichfield over income from the parish, with the mother house of Combermere over tithes, and with Slaidburn also over tithes.

The outline of foundations of the church remains, but there is much more of the monastic buildings. The cloister lay to the south, and walls of its eastern range show that there was a sacristy, a vestibule, a parlour and slype and book-cupboard recesses. The foundations of an octagonal chapter-house can also be seen. The monks' dorter extended over the east range, and beyond it, almost overhanging the river Calder, was their reredorter. The western range, completed in 1415, was scarcely used by the lay brothers. Its undercroft would have been used as a store, the upper floor as a guest-house.

The infirmary block and various buildings were incorporated into a mansion by the Asshetons in the late sixteenth and seventeenth centuries, rebuilt in 1840, and now form the core of the Diocesan Conference Centre. Two gatehouses, early fourteenth-century and late fifteenth-century, survive.

Leicestershire

ULVERSCROFT PRIORY   Augustinian
5 miles south-southwest of Loughborough, off a minor road between B587 and B5330. Ruins privately owned and not open to the public but can be seen from a nearby public footpath.

Ulverscroft Priory was founded in 1134 in a quiet valley among the hills of

Charnwood Forest. The fifteenth-century west tower of the church dominates. Much of the south wall of the nave survives, with tall traceried Perpendicular windows. The chancel has gone, and there were no transepts. Part of the frater south of the cloister can be identified. In the west range the prior's lodging and the monastic guest-house were incorporated into a post-Dissolution house.

Lincolnshire

BOURNE PRIORY   Augustinian
In the small town of Bourne. Nave in parochial use.

Founded in 1138, Bourne Priory acquired abbey status but never became rich or important. Four bays of the Norman church survive as the present parish church, but all monastic buildings have gone. Only a small amount of blank arcading north-west of the church shows where the cloister west range joined it.

CROYLAND ABBEY   Benedictine
In Crowland, 10 miles south of Spalding. The abbey and town use different spellings of the name. North aisle of nave of church in parochial use.

The abbey was founded in 716 to mark the place on a fen island where St Guthlac lived a desolate life. Successive refoundations culminated in the building of the third monastery on the site early in the twelfth century. Much of it was destroyed in an earthquake in 1118. Further rebuilding followed a fire in 1143.

In the second quarter of the fifteenth century the parochial north aisle received its west tower. Adjoining it to the south is the west front of the ruined nave of the monastic church, with its massive, empty west window surrounded by twenty-two beautifully sculptured figures, probably of the fifteenth century. The quatrefoil above the west door illustrates scenes from the life of St Guthlac.

The ruined nave is largely Perpendicular, with a surviving Norman arch of

Croyland Abbey, Lincolnshire: part of the former nave is now the parish church.

the crossing-tower and a carved roodscreen beneath. Nothing remains of any claustral buildings which lay to the south, but in the town the fourteenth-century Triangular Bridge, formerly crossing three streams, since diverted, may have been built by Croyland monks.

DEEPING ST JAMES PRIORY   Benedictine
In the small town of Deeping St James. In parochial use.
    This priory was founded in 1139 as a cell of Thorney Abbey. The church is unusually large, with a sumptuous, seven-bay, late Norman arcade and a long chancel. The west tower dates from 1730. The exterior appearance does not prepare you for the Norman surprises inside.

FREISTON PRIORY   Benedictine
In Freiston, 3 miles east of Boston. Nave of church in parochial use.
    Freiston Priory was founded from Croyland in 1114. Nothing remains except the nine-bay nave, mainly Norman, of the conventual church.

KIRKSTEAD ABBEY   Cistercian
1 mile south of Woodhall Spa. Earthworks and one tall crag of masonry, plus a complete capella ante portas (chapel at the gate), in parochial use. Normally locked, but key available at nearby house.
    Lonely amid the unexcavated earthworks of the vanished abbey, St Leonard's Chapel is an architectural gem of the early thirteenth century, calm, simple, delightful in the purity of its vaulting, its capitals, its arcading and its lancets.

SEMPRINGHAM   Gilbertine
8 miles north of Bourne, off B1177. The church of the earlier of two priories survives in parochial use.
    Sempringham is the birthplace of the Gilbertines, founded here in 1139. Gilbert had earlier built a dwelling and cloister adjoining the north wall of the parish church, for seven maidens who sought a religious life. The Norman nave and four-bay north arcade of Gilbert's church survive, together with an impressive south doorway, with medieval iron scrollwork on the door.
    To the west of this is the site of Gilbert's double priory for canons and nuns, which survived to the Dissolution, when its occupants were described as living blameless lives. Afterwards a mansion was built on the site; it was never occupied and has vanished.

THORNTON ABBEY   Augustinian
10 miles north-east of Scunthorpe on minor road north of A160. English Heritage. Open, grounds daily; gatehouse, afternoon of third Sunday of month.
    Founded as a priory in 1139, Thornton was elevated to abbey status nine years later. Remote from mainstream history but well endowed, it became one of the wealthiest and largest houses of the order. Extensive rebuilding from 1264 continued for over a century. Unrest at the time of the Peasants' Revolt in 1381 encouraged the abbot to rebuild and fortify the gatehouse to provide comfortable rooms for himself and guests, away from the rest of the monastery. Built of bricks from Hull, dressed with stone from near Tadcaster, this largest of monastic gatehouses has main rooms on two floors, reached by a spiral stair in the south-east turret. Wall passages have cabinets and garderobes; the outer façade has sculpture and arrow slits, the eastern one turrets and oriels.
    Extensive earthworks cover over 70 acres (28 hectares), but there are few remains of other monastic buildings except for two exquisitely arcaded walls of the octagonal chapter-house, and part of the treasury and slype.

London

BISHOPSGATE: ST HELEN'S   Benedictine nuns

Between Bishopsgate Street and St Mary Axe. Church in parochial use.

Founded in 1258, St Helen's is interesting because the whole of the church survives, with a double nave. The nuns attached their church and its claustral buildings to the nave of an existing parish church.

LONDON CHARTERHOUSE   Carthusian

In Charterhouse Square. Part is a boys' public school, part an almshouse. It can be visited by prior permission from the Registrar.

The Charterhouse was founded in 1371, but very little of the original monastic structure survives. The site of the chapter-house now has a chapel. There are parts of a cloister wall, entrances into three of the monks' houses, and a few monastic outbuildings absorbed in modern property. The fifteenth-century gatehouse has later upper storeys.

SMITHFIELD PRIORY   Augustinian

North of St Bartholomew's Hospital. In parochial use.

The priory was founded in 1123. The present Norman building was the choir and transepts of the monastery whose nave is now occupied by the present churchyard. The east cloister walk is restored, together with a gatehouse to the west.

St Helen's, Bishopsgate, London: the nuns' squint and the Easter sepulchre.

SOUTHWARK PRIORY-CATHEDRAL

Augustinian

Near the southern end of London Bridge. In episcopal use.

The priory was founded in 1106. Surviving parts of the thirteenth-century church, much restored, are the choir and retro-choir, transepts and tower. The nave is modern. The whole situation, below street level and hemmed in, is rather claustrophobic.

WESTMINSTER ABBEY

Benedictine

Near the Houses of Parliament. In church use as a royal peculiar, neither episcopal nor parochial.

Westminster Abbey was founded by Edward the Confessor, who started building about 1050. What we see now dates from the mid thirteenth century (chancel, crossing and eastern bays). The nave was largely rebuilt in 1375–1400. Henry VII's Chapel was added in 1500–20, and the two west towers in the eighteenth century. Historic, moving, architecturally fascinating and often lovely, it is cluttered with memorials.

The arcaded cloisters to the south are rich in monuments. The great octagonal chapter-house retains its original tiled floor. Beyond it, the east walk leads into the Dark Cloister, a passage between the frater undercroft and dorter. Another passage leads to the Little Cloister, stylistically seventeenth-century. The dorter serves as the great hall of Westminster School, which was founded about twenty years after the Dissolution.

Southwark Cathedral: the east end and tower.

Norfolk

BINHAM PRIORY Benedictine

Half a mile north-west of Binham village, 4 miles south-east of Wells-next-the-Sea by minor road. Nave of church in parochial use. Remainder, together with extensive claustral ruins, English Heritage, freely open.

Binham Priory was founded in 1091. The early priors were not good administrators and the community tended to be disobedient. However, it did acquire property in twenty-one Norfolk parishes.

From a distance the church seems huge, and seven of the original nine bays of the nave, now in parochial use, date from 1130–70, the west front from nearly a century later. Its west window, now largely bricked in, contains very early bar tracery. The chancel and other eastern parts were demolished in 1540, but there are extensive ruins of the crossing.

The monastic quarters south of the church cover a large area. Most of their layout can be appreciated from a raised bank to the west and, although only low flint walls are seen, the important parts are identified by discreet metal labels.

CASTLE ACRE PRIORY Cluniac

A quarter of a mile west of Castle Acre village, 5 miles north of Swaffham. English Heritage. Open throughout the year, except Monday and Tuesday, November to March.

The ruins of Castle Acre Priory, founded by William Warenne, Earl of Surrey, in 1089 as a daughter house of Lewes, are the most extensive Cluniac survival in Britain. As with other 'alien priories', Castle Acre suffered from royal taxation and various restrictions during the fourteenth-century French wars.

Most of the church has gone, although its plan reveals a seven-bay nave with aisles, transepts with apsidal chapels, and a three-bay presbytery. The surviving west front is a late Norman *tour de force* with three doorways, round-headed

Castle Acre Priory, Norfolk: the brick and flint gatehouse.

Creake Abbey, Norfolk: the chancel and the transept arches.

windows, blind and interlaced arcading and the remains of a huge Perpendicular window. The south tower still stands to four-storey height, its upper stage having Early English windows. Cliff-like walls of flint and stone hint at the glory of the former nave.

Claustral buildings to the south followed the usual plan: book cupboard, chapter-house, undercroft of dorter, dorter stairs and dorter with windows and some arcading. Beyond, at right angles, is a well-preserved reredorter, 91 feet (28 metres) long, with river and drain tunnelled beneath. Fragments of frater, kitchen and infirmary walls survive.

In the west range the prior built a splendid residence for himself about 1500 – the roofed building which adjoins the south-west corner of the west front. An earlier, vaulted undercroft supports spacious rooms above, together with a chapel and altar recess, two oriel windows and a brick and timber gable, the whole similar to a Tudor manor house, commodious and comfortable. The contemporary two-storey gatehouse is of brick and flint.

CREAKE ABBEY
Augustinian
8 miles north-west of Fakenham, 1 mile north of North Creake, off B1355. English Heritage. Freely open at all reasonable times.

Creake Abbey was founded in 1189 as a priory but elevated by Henry III to abbey status in 1231. Secretive, sad, quietly holy and a little gem, Creake never housed more than seven canons. It suffered from bad luck, with fires in 1378 and 1490, when the canons demolished the nave and transepts and walled off the west end of the crossing. In 1500 plague killed the canons, but the abbot survived until 1506, when the abbey ceased, over thirty years before the Dissolution.

High flint walls of parts of the late-thirteenth-century church survive, mainly the east and west arches of the crossing, chancel walls to considerable height, some doorways, the high south wall of the nave and a lower north wall.

Thetford Priory, Norfolk.

NORWICH CATHEDRAL-PRIORY
Benedictine

In the city centre, off Wensum Street. In use as an episcopal cathedral.

Founded in 1095–6, Norwich Priory became a monastic cathedral five years later. The Norman ground plan is the least changed of any English cathedral. Contemporary with Durham, the architectural effect is much more delicate because of the treatment of the nave piers. The apsed chancel has an ambulatory with projecting chapels; chancel and transept roofs had timber replaced by stone vaults in the late fifteenth and early sixteenth centuries.

The cloisters are the most impressive survival, rebuilt between 1297 (east walk) and 1430 (west walk), the window tracery clearly indicating architectural progress. An unusual upper storey, now used for storage and choristers' rooms, was probably built for winter use. On the south range, some arcaded frater walls stand to a good height.

The precinct was approached from the town by two gates. The Great Gate, St Ethelbert's, dates from 1316. Its upper parts were restored in 1806. To its north, the Erpingham Gate, buttressed and richly sculptured, is a century later. The fifteenth-century Water Gate, by Pull's Ferry, guarded the canal approach from the river Wensum, by which stone was brought to build the cathedral.

THETFORD PRIORY
Cluniac

On the western edge of Thetford, near the station. English Heritage. Freely open at all reasonable times.

Founded in 1103–4, Thetford Priory was colonised by monks from Lewes ten years later. The fragmented ruins, set among secluded lawns, have been excavated to reveal a plan similar to that at Castle Acre. Some imagination is needed to envisage what the buildings were like. One detached structure west of the northern end of the west claustral range may have been the prior's lodge. To the north-west the fourteenth-century gatehouse, faced in knapped flint, is the most impressive survival, turreted, but without roof or parapet.

Walsingham Priory, Norfolk: the east wall of the chancel.

WALSINGHAM PRIORY
Augustinian

In the centre of Little Walsingham, 5 miles north-northeast of Fakenham. Privately owned, but open daily, April to October and at other times. Fee payable.

In 1051 the lady of the manor saw a vision here of the Virgin Mary. It was repeated, and in response to its apparent request a replica of the Holy House at Nazareth was built. Most medieval English monarchs visited the shrine, and Walsingham became an important place of pilgrimage. In 1169 the priory was founded, becoming one of the richest in East Anglia.

All that survives amid the smooth lawn of the eighteenth-century house called Walsingham Abbey is the tall east wall of the fourteenth-century chancel, with twin turrets and a huge empty window between. To its east a re-erected Norman doorway leads to muddy-looking healing wells. Fragments of conventual buildings can be identified at the rear of the mansion, where the dorter undercroft (called a crypt on the notices) can be visited. A fifteenth-century gatehouse faces High Street and is the present entrance to the precinct.

WYMONDHAM ABBEY
Benedictine

On the western edge of Wymondham, off B1135, 9 miles south-west of Norwich. Church in parochial use.

Founded as a priory in 1107, it became an abbey in 1449. Its church is the only monastic survival and is dominated by two tall axial towers, whose competing heights illustrate centuries of quarrel between the priory and the townsfolk. The monks built the crossing-tower in 1390–1400, adding a solid west wall across its nave arch where the present reredos is. Fifty years later the defiant townsfolk built their own dignified west tower in Perpendicular style. The mid twelfth-century Norman nave between has been much changed, with many blocked arches and arcades. The north aisle represents a parochial widening contemporary with the west tower, the south aisle being added a century later.

Canons Ashby, Northamptonshire: part of the priory church is now St Mary's church.

Northamptonshire

CANONS ASHBY PRIORY   Augustinian
7 miles west of Towcester. Part of the priory church in parochial use.

Only fragments of the priory church, founded about 1150 in the gentle landscape of the south-west of the county, survive – two bays of the early thirteenth-century nave and north aisle, with the north-west tower added about 1350. A fine western portal has good arcading on each side. The conventual buildings were converted to a private house after the Dissolution, but this stood for only a few years. To the north-east, in a field, is the former small monastic well-house, with a pitched roof, tunnel-vaulted inside.

Northumberland

BLANCHLAND ABBEY   Premonstratensian
13 miles south-southeast of Hexham, in the Derwent valley, west of the reservoir, by B6306. Part of the church in parochial use. Other monastic buildings in current use.

Founded in 1165, Blanchland's history is restricted to the early fourteenth century and the last fifty years before the Dissolution. Its remote situation, and various Scottish campaigns, led to financial difficulties. Blanchland has the only Premonstratensian church still in use, and the site of the abbey and many of its monastic buildings are uniquely preserved in the present, extremely attractive village.

The church had an aisleless nave whose south wall is now the south wall of the churchyard. The north transept, with a tower adjoining its northern end, and the chancel survive in use. There was no south transept. The west range of the claustral buildings is now incorporated into the Lord Crewe Hotel and includes the abbot's lodging, the guest-house and the monastic kitchen.

The abbot's lodging was almost certainly a late-thirteenth- or early-fourteenth-century pele-tower and retains its vaulted undercroft. The gatehouse probably dates from 1500.

The whole of the monastic estate came into the ownership of the trustees of Lord Crewe, Bishop of Durham, in 1752, and almost all the houses round the two squares of the present village represent the mid-eighteenth-century rebuilding for lead-miners at the extensive Lord Crewe lead mines in the surrounding hills. In this layout they appear to echo part of the earlier claustral plan, those on the south probably occupying the site of the frater.

BRINKBURN PRIORY   Augustinian
4¹/2 miles south-east of Rothbury off B6334, reached by a short woodland walk from a car park. English Heritage. Open daily, April to October.

Founded in 1135 and exquisitely situated within a loop of the river Coquet, Brinkburn never became wealthy. As a result, the church was little changed after its completion, so it retains a rare architectural purity of the late twelfth and early thirteenth centuries. It was sensitively restored by Thomas Austin in 1858 and is a superb example of the transition from Romanesque to Gothic. The north door is exuberant in its late Norman detail, with a delicate arcade above of three trefoiled arches. Round-headed windows above and a lancet below at the east give way to lancets in the six-bay nave and transepts.

Of the cloister, a few blank arches survive against the south side of the nave. Scarcely any other monastic buildings remain, having been merged into a late Georgian and Romantic castellated mansion.

HEXHAM PRIORY (now Abbey)   Augustinian
In the centre of Hexham. Church in parochial use.

Founded in 674 by St Wilfrid, Hexham Priory became a cathedral four years later. It was refounded for Augustinian canons in 1113, suffered repeatedly in Scottish raids and was later caught up in the Wars of the Roses. The last prior helped to initiate the Pilgrimage of Grace in 1536.

Hexham Abbey, Northumberland.

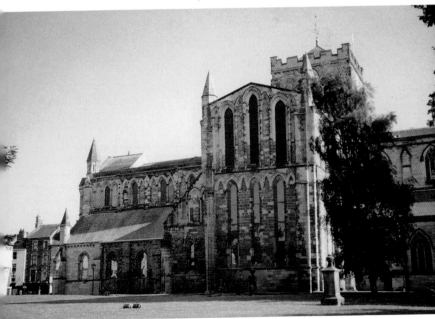

The most historically eloquent part of the church is Wilfrid's crypt, reached by steps below the nave. Constructed of Roman masonry from nearby *Corstopitum,* it is the finest Anglo-Saxon crypt in England. The present church is essentially of two periods, with the choir, crossing and transepts largely of the 1180–1250 building, characteristically Early English in style with tall graceful pointed arches and delicate lancets. The south transept contains a unique survival, the monks' night stair, a wide, well-trodden flight of steps leading to their dormitory. A poor restoration of 1858 had a new nave added in 1907–10, in the Early English style, and contains many sculptured fragments, from Roman to medieval, including the remains of a stone pulpitum.

Much of the priory precinct is now hidden by later buildings. The cloister was south of the nave, and its west walk shows seven gabled blank arches of the lavatorium. The chapter-house vestibule survives as a small chapel with a modern roof. To the north of the priory is the prior's gate of 1160.

HULNE PRIORY   Carmelite
2 miles north-west of Alnwick, in Hulne Park. Free permit for access to Hulne Park, pedestrian only, from the Estate Office, Alnwick Castle. Open end of April to early October.

The substantial ruins of Hulne Priory, founded in 1242, lie deeply secluded in the Duke of Northumberland's vast park above the valley of the river Aln. A rare complete curtain wall surrounds the precinct, with the main gate on the south leading to the outer court. The south wall of the nave and chancel survives almost intact, with sacristy and chapter-house, part of the cloister and a gable of the dorter. Much remains of the infirmary, but an unusual addition is the late-fifteenth-century tower built on the west of the cloister garth, a defensive structure in perilous times. In 1776 the first Duke added an elegant Gothic summerhouse. The whole group in its Arcadian setting is memorably beautiful.

LINDISFARNE PRIORY   Benedictine
On Holy Island, 6 miles east of A1, accessible at low tide across a causeway, with tide tables posted at each end. English Heritage. Open daily throughout the year.

Awe-inspiring in its religious and historical context, its setting on a low and formerly lonely island makes Lindisfarne the most evocative of all Britain's monastic ruins. It was founded by King Oswald of Northumbria for St Aidan in 634, when it was settled by Celtic monks from Iona, but abandoned in 875 after eighty years of Danish raids. Its monks carried with them the body and sacred relics of St Cuthbert, finally reaching Durham, where they built the first cathedral church, about 995. In 1083 the Norman bishop decided to refound Lindisfarne Priory as a dependent house.

Most of the ruins of the priory church date from the first half of the twelfth century, their red sandstone masonry curiously weathered. The west front, with a fine portal, survives to a considerable height, as do the north wall of the nave and the two eastern bays of the north aisle arcade. Two of the massive crossing piers survive to support the famous 'rainbow' arch, a delicate diagonal span. The west wall of the north transept and the east wall of the south transept stand to a good height, together with much of the mid-twelfth-century chancel, whose large east window was a later insertion. Beyond the southern end of the west front is a tall turret with an internal spiral staircase leading to crossbow loops over the portal. A similar turret to the north has almost completely gone, but their existence hints at Lindisfarne's concern about Scottish raids.

Monastic buildings are mainly of the thirteenth and fourteenth centuries. The cloister to the south, initially square, later extended to a rectangle, but only low walls remain. The fireplace and chimney of the warming-house and the prior's

Tynemouth Priory, Northumberland, lies within the walls of the castle, overlooking the river Tyne.

house are preserved. The west range retains in its west wall the remains of six lancet windows. Cellars, pantry, kitchen and brewhouse had a barbican to their south, with the remains of a battlemented wall beyond with a gatehouse, enclosing an outer court.

TYNEMOUTH PRIORY   Benedictine
In Tynemouth, near the North Pier. English Heritage. Open daily except Mondays and Tuesdays, November to March.
The priory was founded in 1089 after two earlier foundations had been destroyed by Danes. On its exposed promontory the priory lay within the walls of a Norman castle, but from the end of the eleventh century it enjoyed the unique situation of owning the fortifications. It suffered from frequent Scottish attacks, some Northumbrian ones, and regular demands for hospitality, particularly by Edward III, who during the Scottish wars insisted on maintaining a garrison there. By the end of the fourteenth century the massive medieval walls had to be rebuilt, including the gate tower, and were completed soon after 1400. With a perimeter of 3200 feet (975 metres), Tynemouth Priory/Castle was one of the largest fortified areas in Britain. The huge gatehouse with barbican marks its landward entrance.

Little of the Norman church stands to any height, and it is the Early English additions of the late twelfth century that create the greatest impact. The whole of the east wall of the chancel, together with three bays of its south wall, soars skywards, with tall lancets, a vesica window, blank arcading along the plinth, and groups of seven shafts separating the windows. Beneath the east wall was the last addition to the priory, the mid-fifteenth-century Percy Chantry, a low, roofed chamber with detailed vaulting and thirty-three sculptured bosses.

Nottinghamshire

BLYTH PRIORY   Benedictine
12 miles south of Doncaster, by A634, near A1. Church in parochial use.
Beautifully situated on the village green, only part of the church of the priory, founded in 1088, survives, the south aisle of its nave having been enlarged for parochial use in 1290.

Five bays of the original seven possess a rugged, uncompromising early

Norman severity. The present east wall may contain part of the original pulpitum, but the crossing, transepts and chancel have gone, together with the monastic buildings.

MATTERSEY PRIORY Gilbertines
7 miles north of East Retford, 1 mile east of Mattersey village, south of A631. English Heritage. Freely open at all reasonable times, reached by a rough track.

This small priory was founded in 1185 by the west bank of the river Idle and largely destroyed by fire in 1279. The fragmented, though evocative, ruins are now surrounded by farmland. Parts of the original church walls remain, but the best-preserved ruins are those of the aisled frater, with kitchen and serving hatch, part of a cloister and the remnant of a later tower.

NEWSTEAD PRIORY Augustinian
5½ miles south of Mansfield, west of A60. 12 miles north of Nottingham. Nottingham City Council. Mansion open daily, April to September. Grounds open all year.

The priory was founded about 1170. After the Dissolution it passed to the Byron family, who over the next two centuries adapted the monastic buildings into a mansion, now known as Newstead Abbey. Much more was done in the early nineteenth century, and Newstead is a rare example where the claustral complex can still be identified within such a conversion, including the south transept of the church, the chapter-house, warming-room, frater, kitchen and prior's lodging. The cloisters surround a garden.

The nineteenth-century remodelling of the west claustral range is aligned with the west front of the priory church, a beautiful, late thirteenth-century façade in three parts with the remains of a graceful six-light window, crowned by a gable above.

RUFFORD ABBEY Cistercian
2 miles south of Ollerton, east of A614. English Heritage and Nottinghamshire County Council, in Rufford Country Park. Open daily.

Rufford Abbey was founded in 1146 on infertile and difficult land in Sherwood Forest, where the monks felled and sold timber, grazed sheep and sold wool. After being suppressed in 1536, the monastic estate passed to the Earl of Shrewsbury and subsequently to Bess of Hardwick, who built a large Elizabethan house on the site of the church and cloisters. More changes were made in the next two centuries, and after army occupation during the Second World War most of the buildings were demolished.

Rufford Abbey, Nottinghamshire: the cellarium.

Thurgarton Priory, Nottinghamshire: the surviving west tower on the parish church.

The undercroft of the west claustral range has been restored; part cellarium and part the lay brothers' frater, it is vaulted and well preserved. It is hoped eventually to mark out the site of the cloister and church.

THURGARTON PRIORY   Augustinian
3¹/₂ miles south of Southwell. Part of church in parochial use.

Thurgarton Priory was founded in 1140. The three western bays of the early thirteenth-century church survive, together with one of a fine pair of west towers almost equalling those of nearby Southwell Minster, and a superb west portal. Three of the priory misericords are in the present chancel.

WORKSOP PRIORY   Augustinian
East of the centre of Worksop. Formerly known as Radford Priory. In parochial use.

The priory was founded about 1119, but almost all that remains is the long nave, mainly late Norman, of the second church. To this was added in 1250 an exquisite Lady Chapel, which became isolated and roofless after the Dissolution but was restored and rejoined to the nave when a new south transept was built in 1929. A late Norman doorway from the nave to the now vanished cloister also survives. The twin west towers, apart from their parapets, are also Norman.

South of the church is the beautiful fourteenth-century gatehouse, Worksop's most handsome building, with a broad, arched gateway, with oriel above, and an outside staircase.

Dorchester Abbey, Oxfordshire: a capital carved with the figures of sleeping monks.

Oxfordshire

ABINGDON ABBEY   Benedictine
In Abingdon. Fragmented remains, partly incorporated into other buildings in the townscape.

Founded in 964 , the abbey prospered, with the town at its gates, largely on its medieval wool trade. Most of the abbey was destroyed at the Dissolution, and of the remaining buildings the late fifteenth-century gatehouse is the best, with its pointed arches, traceried spandrels, niches, windows and battlements. Abbey Gardens represent the site of the church; along the riverside is a range of former monastic buildings. The thirteenth-century Chequer Hall may have been the abbey's business office. Above it soars the most interesting medieval chimney stack in England, with vents at the top in the form of stepped lancets.

DORCHESTER ABBEY   Augustinian
In Dorchester-on-Thames. The monastic church incorporates the present parish church.

One of the earliest in England, the abbey was founded in 634 and refounded for Augustinian canons in 1140. At the Dissolution almost all the monastic buildings north of the church were demolished, but the church was bought and given to the parish. Most of the north wall of the twelfth-century church remains. Additions made in the fourteenth century included a magnificent and architecturally original choir with splendid sculpture and tracery, including the beautiful Jesse window.

The fifteenth-century Old School House, west of the abbey, may have been the monastic guest-house.

OXFORD, CHRISTCHURCH CATHEDRAL   Augustinian
(formerly St Frideswide's Priory)
In Oxford. Conventual church became a cathedral and Christ Church college chapel in 1546.

St Frideswide's was founded first as a nunnery in 727, burnt down in 1002 and rebuilt twice afterwards. The present structure, late twelfth-century, survived the Reformation by becoming Wolsey's and Henry VIII's college chapel. Extensive restorations were carried out in the 1870s.

Haughmond Abbey, Shropshire: the site of the infirmary.

Of the monastic remains, the south walk of the cloister is original, together with parts of the north and east walks, mainly of about 1500. The chapter-house is largely early thirteenth-century but retains a Norman doorway, and the frater is now used for college rooms.

Shropshire

BROMFIELD PRIORY   Benedictine
3 miles north-west of Ludlow, off A49. Church in parochial use.
The priory was founded in 1155. The nave of the priory church survives, shorn of transepts and chancel. There are no claustral remains, but the priory gatehouse to the north survives, stone below with fourteenth-century timbering above.

BUILDWAS ABBEY   Cistercian
On the south bank of the river Severn, on B4578, 2 miles west of Ironbridge. English Heritage. Open April to September.
This was founded as a Savignac abbey in 1135 and absorbed into the Cistercian order in 1147. Except for its roof and aisle walls, the remarkably intact church is a typical, modest, early Cistercian construction, simple yet noble, with a seven-bay nave on stocky round piers and a clerestory above with round-headed windows. A severe, square-ended chancel is slightly later.

Of the monastic buildings which lay to the north, the east claustral range has a fine chapter-house, rib-vaulted and roofed, with a groin-vaulted crypt, a sacristy-cum-library, a parlour and the dorter undercroft. To the north-east, the infirmary and part of the abbot's house have been incorporated into a private house.

HAUGHMOND ABBEY   Augustinian
3 miles north-east of Shrewsbury, off B5062. English Heritage. Open April to September.
Founded about 1135 as a priory for Augustinian canons, Haughmond was

largely rebuilt in the late twelfth century. A westwards-sloping site at the foot of a wooded escarpment has resulted in an unusual monastic plan based on a double cloister on a north-south axis.

The southern approach misleads. It is best to go to the northern limit of the site, where only low foundation walls of the church survive. South of the nave is the first cloister, with the inner wall of the west range showing two huge arcades of a lavatorium. Opposite is the chapter-house, with three arches sumptuously carved, and a wooden Tudor ceiling inside. Further fragments of the east range are beyond this.

The second or infirmary cloister is to the south. Its south range contains the best of Haughmond, the infirmary and abbot's lodging. The former has a fine row of two-light windows, early thirteenth-century, and a great window flanked by two turrets in the west wall. To the east, the abbot's lodging is dominated by its six-light, late-fifteenth-century bay window. This is the façade seen first by the visitor and was completed before the Dissolution.

LILLESHALL ABBEY   Augustinian
On an unclassified road off A518, 4 miles north of Oakengates. English Heritage. Open April to September.

There are substantial remains of the large church, with aisleless nave, four-bay presbytery and south transept. The processional doorway from the nave into the cloister is ornately decorated, and to its south is a two-compartment book locker. Beyond this, on the east range, are the sacristy, slype and chapter-house with walls standing. Surviving walls of the south range show that in the fourteenth century it was divided into two, the western half a frater, the eastern one a warming-house.

SHREWSBURY ABBEY   Benedictine monks
In Abbey Foregate, east of English Bridge, Shrewsbury. Norman nave used as a parish church.

The original Norman nave piers and arcades survive, together with other arches and doorways, but much aesthetic damage was done in restorations of 1862 and 1886. Telford destroyed most of the monastic buildings with his London–Holyhead road of 1836, but the elegant refectory pulpit survives by the side of a large car park south of the east end of the nave.

Lilleshall Abbey, the east processional doorway and a book-locker recess.

WENLOCK PRIORY   Cluniac monks
In the town of Much Wenlock, just off A458. English Heritage. Open daily
throughout the year.
Founded by Leofric, Earl of Mercia, about 1050 on the site of a Saxon
nunnery, the priory was colonised by monks from France thirty years later.
Their numbers remained remarkably consistent at around forty almost to the
Dissolution.
Almost all the large remains are of the church, with early-thirteenth-century
transept walls standing to considerable height. An unusual small rectangular
chamber occupies three western bays of the nave triforium and was probably a
chapel. Architecturally outstanding are the intersecting arches which form
blind arcading of the chapter-house walls, and the beautiful sculpture, 1180–90,
of the unusual free-standing lavatorium close to the south walk of the cloister,
which had pairs of columned arcades surrounding a central well.
In the fifteenth century an infirmary and prior's lodge were built to the south
and east of the south transept. These were converted into a private house after
the Dissolution and remain so today.

WHITE LADIES PRIORY   Augustinian canonesses
Off an unclassified road between A5 and A41, 8 miles north-west of Wolver-
hampton. English Heritage. Freely open at all times.
There are very meagre ruins of a late Norman church, with an aisleless nave
and square-ended presbytery. It was converted to a house after the Dissolution,
and Charles II hid there and in nearby woods in 1651 before moving to
Boscobel House.

Somerset

BATH ABBEY   Benedictine
In the centre of Bath. Church in parochial use, sharing an episcopal see with
Wells.
Bath Abbey was founded in 676 for nuns, who were replaced by monks in
758. After being destroyed by Danes and refounded in 963, the abbey was
subsequently sacked in 1087 and refounded with a new community the following year. It became a cathedral-priory in 1107, but by 1476 the buildings were
dilapidated, and so a new church was begun in 1499, occupying only the nave
area of its predecessor. Conventual buildings were not rebuilt and the new
church was not completed by the time of the Dissolution. It was offered to the
city for 500 marks (£333), but the citizens turned down the offer. The building
was gutted and its shell allowed to become ruinous. It passed into private hands,
and in 1560 Edmund Colthurst gave it to the city for use as the parish church. A
long period of renovation was largely concluded by 1616. Although the choir
vault had been completed a century earlier than this, the nave vault was not
finished until 1869, so that the beautiful building seen today shows how later
generations tried to follow the original ideas of the early-sixteenth-century
architects.

CLEEVE ABBEY   Cistercian
In Washford, 2 miles south-west of Watchet, off A39. English Heritage. Open
all the year.
Cleeve Abbey was founded in 1198. Although the church has gone, Cleeve
has the most complete Cistercian conventual buildings in England, with the east
and south ranges retaining roofs and floors, having been saved at the Dissolution by the Luttrells of Dunster Castle, who turned it into a house and farm.
The cloister lay to the south of the nave, its thirteenth-century east range

Cleeve Abbey, Somerset: the thirteenth-century gatehouse.

remarkably complete, with sacristy, vestibule to the chapter-house, day stairs to the dorter, parlour and slype, and then the southern half of the dorter undercroft used by the monks as a heated common room. The dorter above, 137 feet (42 metres) long, which could accommodate thirty monks, retains its walls, door and lancet windows.

The original frater lay parallel to this, extending north-south from the south range. Of this nothing is left but its thirteenth-century tiled floor. It was replaced in the early sixteenth century by the last abbot, William Dovell, who turned it on to an east-west axis and subdivided its ground floor into two rooms, including a kitchen. The new frater is comparable with a medieval great hall, with a splendid wagon roof and traceried windows. To its west are smaller rooms, one with wall-paintings. In the cloister north walk is a rare example of the abbot's collation seat, an arched recess in its north wall. The thirteenth-century gatehouse was also altered by Abbot Dovell.

DUNSTER PRIORY   Benedictine
In Dunster village, 2 miles south-east of Minehead. Church in parochial use.

The priory was founded in 1090. The fifteenth- and sixteenth-century church survives and retains a Norman doorway in the west front. There are scarcely any remains of priory buildings. There is a round sixteenth-century dovecote nearby, a contemporary barn to the east; in Conduit Lane a stone-built sixteenth-century well-house was probably the priory's water supply.

GLASTONBURY ABBEY   Benedictine
In the centre of Glastonbury. Privately owned, but fee-paying public access all the year.

A Saxon foundation, achieving tenth-century greatness under the abbacy of St Dunstan, this largest and wealthiest of English abbeys is singularly disappointing. Most of the huge church, rebuilt between 1189 and 1220 after a disastrous fire, has gone, although three bays of the south aisle wall stand, with the eastern piers of the crossing, and fragments of transept walls and arches. The elaborately ornate late Norman Lady Chapel survives as a shell, near the west end of the church, and shows superb carving.

Low masonry walls and a few piers are all that remain of the claustral buildings. The complete abbot's kitchen, probably late fourteenth-century, survives as one of the best-preserved of English medieval kitchens, square in plan but with corner fireplaces giving it an octagonal interior, capped by an octagonal pyramid roof with lantern.

The abbey gatehouse faces Market Street, and in High Street the stone-built Tribunal (English Heritage) was the abbey's fifteenth-century courthouse. Nearby is the George and Pilgrims Inn, built by the abbey probably in the late fifteenth century, while at Meare, 3 miles north-west by B3151, the Abbot's Fish House (English Heritage, key from Manor House Farm), built about 1340, was the fisherman's house where fish for the abbey was salted and stored.

HINTON CHARTERHOUSE   Carthusian
5¹/₂ miles south-southeast of Bath, by A36. Privately owned. No public access.

Founded in 1232 by Ela, widow of William Longespée, Hinton was the second Carthusian house. The remains, which can be seen from the road, consist of the tall thirteenth-century chapter-house with adjoining sacristy, roofed and well preserved. The vaulted room above the chapter-house, with lancet windows, was the library. To the west are the remains of the frater, above a vaulted undercroft; parts of the former guest-house are incorporated into a later mansion. Excavations have revealed the outline of the great cloister, 226 feet (69 metres) square, with fourteen cells around it.

MUCHELNEY ABBEY   Benedictine
In Muchelney, 3 miles south of Langport, by minor road. English Heritage. Open daily, April to October.

The abbey was founded in 693 and refounded in 939. There are outlines of a late Norman church and cloister, which have been excavated. Only in the south claustral range are there any significant remains, with the frater north wall and abbot's lodging forming a fine group of early-sixteenth-century buildings. From a low anteroom off the cloister a stone stair leads to the abbot's parlour with its sumptuous fireplace surmounted by a richly decorated frieze. Large, traceried south windows illuminate a light room, from which three other rooms lead, all with fine ceilings, some with wall-paintings. The southern extension of the east cloister range still has its reredorter, with slit windows, and, below its west wall, five discharging openings.

WITHAM PRIORY   Carthusian
6 miles south-southwest of Frome, by minor road east off A350. Church in parochial use.

This was the first English Carthusian foundation, in 1179. Its third prior, St Hugh of Lincoln, was responsible for the permanent buildings. The austere, aisleless and rib-vaulted church, three bays long, had a fourth western one added in 1876, as well as heavy flying buttresses and a bellcote to replace the west tower. In the village the former monastic dovecote is now a parish room.

WOODSPRING PRIORY   Augustinian
3 miles north of Weston-super-Mare, reached by minor roads and farm track. Now owned by the Landmark Trust and let as a holiday house.

Founded in 1226, this was always a poor house. Part of the small church survives, with a crossing-tower but no chancel or transepts. After the Dissolution it became a dwelling house at the centre of farm buildings. The infirmary and a gatehouse arch also survive.

Croxden Abbey, Staffordshire.

Staffordshire

CROXDEN ABBEY
Cistercian

5 miles north-west of Uttoxeter, off A50, reached by minor roads. English Heritage. Open daily.

Founded in 1178, Croxden became relatively wealthy through sheep-rearing. Unfortunately a road passes across the site and diagonally bisects the church, passing the angle between nave and south transept. All the remaining ruins are to the south of this. The nave's west wall stands to a good height, with tall

Tutbury Priory, Staffordshire: the west door.

Bury St Edmunds Abbey, Suffolk: the Norman tower.

lancets and a four-ordered doorway. Of similar height is the south aisle wall of the nave, together with the south and west walls of the south transept, again with tall lancets of the early thirteenth century. Excavations have shown that five circular chapels radiated from the apsidal eastern end of the church, as occurred in other late Cistercian foundations.

Monastic buildings followed the usual Cistercian pattern, but only the lower walls of the east cloister range and parts of the south range remain intact, including a doorway and two windows of the square chapterhouse. To the south-east of the east range are the remains of the abbot's lodging of 1335. The chapel by the gate was in parochial use until 1885, when it was demolished and replaced by the present St Giles church.

TUTBURY PRIORY   Benedictine
In Tutbury, at the northern edge of the town. Nave and south aisle of church in parochial use.

The priory was founded in 1080, but nothing survives of the monastic buildings. Much of the church was replaced in 1886, and the crossing-tower was rebuilt in the seventeenth century. The original west front of the church is its great glory, a lavish composition of 1160–70 centred on a sumptuously decorated portal of seven orders, one of which includes the earliest English use of alabaster, a local stone. The south aisle doorway is also Norman, its lintel illustrating a boar hunt. The internal view of this western end of the church also shows rich Norman carving.

Suffolk

BURY ST EDMUNDS ABBEY   Benedictine
East of the town centre, off Abbeygate Street. English Heritage. Extensive but low-walled ruins of the abbey church and claustral ranges lie in a public park and cemetery comprising the whole monastic precinct, freely accessible.

Founded in 633, refounded in 1020, the abbey became second in importance to Glastonbury. Early fires led to extensive rebuilding in the second half of the twelfth century. A hundred years later there were eighty monks, twenty-one chaplains and 111 servants. Rioting townsfolk caused much damage in 1327, when the abbot was abducted. The Peasants' Revolt of 1381 brought more trouble, destruction and the looting of abbey treasures. The tower collapsed in 1430, and the whole church and frater were burned in a disastrous fire in 1465, to be rebuilt soon afterwards. The abbey's last fifty years were more peaceful but very little survived the Dissolution in 1539, when the number of monks had

Leiston Abbey, Suffolk: from the south, showing the flushwork on the chapel wall.

declined to forty-five.

Scanty and fragmented remains give only a shadowy hint of former greatness, with meagre ruins of the crossing, transepts, crypt and part of the nave. Houses have been built into the heart of the west front of the church. The Abbot's Bridge and considerable lengths of precinct wall are well preserved, but the best survivals are the two gateways fronting the main street. The taller, southern one is the Norman tower of St James, early twelfth-century, serving as an entrance to the abbey church and as the belfry of the adjoining St James's church. The Great Gate, facing Abbeygate Street, was built between 1327 and 1346 to give access to the great court and abbot's palace. Its upper storey was added between 1353 and 1384.

LEISTON ABBEY   Premonstratensian
4 miles east of Saxmundham, 1 mile north of Leiston, off B1069. English Heritage. Freely open at reasonable times.

The abbey was refounded in 1365 on a new site, 1½ miles inland from the earlier foundation on Minsmere Marshes.

Walls of the chancel, crossing and transepts of the fourteenth-century church stand to considerable height. All three ranges of the claustral buildings contain good walling, some subsequently incorporated into a house. In the sixteenth century a brick gatehouse was added to the west range. The Lady Chapel of the church has been restored and is in ecclesiastical use.

Surrey

CHERTSEY ABBEY   Benedictine
On the northern edge of Chertsey, by Abbey River.

Nothing remains above ground, most masonry having been used in building Henry VIII's Oatlands Palace at Weybridge. Many fine tiles and some coffins from the excavations are now displayed in Chertsey Museum.

NEWARK PRIORY   Augustinian
3 miles east of Woking, by B367.

Newark Priory was founded in 1189, but all that remains on an attractive site

Chertsey Abbey, Surrey: a tile pattern based upon a medieval tile illustrating the legend of Tristan and Isolde, from the collection in Chertsey Museum.

by the river Wey is a good deal of flint walling of the church – the south transept, the north and south walls of the presbytery almost to the vault – and some window and door openings. There are no conventual buildings.

WAVERLEY ABBEY
Cistercian

2 miles south-east of Farnham, off B3001. English Heritage. Freely open at all reasonable times.

The abbey was founded in 1128 as the first Cistercian house in England, but the meagre ruins that remain date from the thirteenth century. Constantly damaged by flooding of the nearby river Wey, the church was not dedicated until 1278, a century after the first church had been completed.

Excavation has revealed the complete ground plan of what Pevsner describes as 'the central power-house for a great deal of English architecture', but the surviving fragments give little hint of this. One end of the monks' dormitory survives to gable height, with some of the side walls. To its west are four vaulted bays of the cellarium, with part of its upper floor and west wall. There are substantial remains only of the south transept of the church, with a high west wall.

Sussex

BATTLE ABBEY
Benedictine

In the town of Battle, at the southern end of High Street. English Heritage. Open daily throughout the year.

Battle Abbey was founded in 1067 by William I to atone for blood shed at the battle of Hastings, with the church altar on the spot where Harold had been

Waverley Abbey, Surrey.

killed. Most of the church has gone, but excavations have revealed much of its plan. Of claustral buildings the roofless shell of the thirteenth-century dormitory stands to considerable height. Beneath it the undercroft is divided into four parts, and there are low ruins of a reredorter. One wall of the frater and some cloister arcading survive, but the chapter-house has gone.

Many of the domestic buildings were converted into a mansion after the Dissolution, altered to the neo-Gothic style in the 1850s; they now form the nucleus of a school. The 1338 gatehouse dominates the precinct entrance from the town, with tall polygonal turrets flanking the main part, and carriage and pedestrian portals beneath.

BAYHAM ABBEY   Premonstratensian

1³/4 miles west of Lamberhurst off B2169. English Heritage. Open daily throughout the year.

Founded in 1208, Bayham Abbey stands in a beautiful setting by the river Teise. The most important parts, with walls to considerable height, are the eastern part of the church and the eastern domestic range.

The early-thirteenth-century church was extended at its eastern end about 1300 and had new transepts built, with transept chapels, the older ones being walled off. The short presbytery has a polygonal eastern end, of which only low walls remain.

A narrow, aisle-less nave shows fifteenth-century rebuilding at its western end, where new arches were inserted into its south wall.

The eastern claustral range has recesses used as book cupboards, remains of the sacristy and chapter-house, and the base of the night stair to the dormitory, with part of the undercroft. Bayham Abbey had two gatehouses, one from Sussex (vanished) and one from Kent, whose fourteenth-century ruins survive, north-west of the church.

Bayham Abbey, Sussex: the north transept.

The abbey ruins were treated as a picturesque feature of an eighteenth-century landscaped park.

BOXGROVE PRIORY — Benedictine
3¹/₂ miles north-east of Chichester. Choir of church in parochial use.

The nave of 1170 was abandoned at the Dissolution by the parishioners, who kept the choir and crossing as their parish church. Transepts are ceiled over to provide upper floors, but Boxgrove's glory is the Early English chancel of four double bays. The vault was painted in the mid sixteenth century.

Little remains of claustral buildings to the north except a chapter-house doorway and, entirely separate, north and south gable walls of the roofless guest-house of 1300.

LEWES PRIORY — Cluniac
At Southover, on the southern edge of the town. Ruins easily seen, beyond fences and wire.

Of the chief house of the Cluniac order in England, founded in 1077, only fragments survive. Ironically, there is a very full account of its demolition in 1538. Among the remains are part of the frater vault, the undercroft of the dormitory and ruins of the gatehouse.

MICHELHAM PRIORY — Augustinian
2¹/₂ miles west of Hailsham, by minor road off A22. Sussex Past. Open daily, March to October.

Founded in 1229, Michelham Priory had become dilapidated before the Dissolution. Incorporated into a Tudor house are part of the frater, including the

Lewes Priory, Sussex: the twelfth-century reredorter.

Michelham Priory, Sussex: the bridge and gatehouse leading to the Tudor house.

lavatorium arches and pulpit stairs, and the southern end of the west range with undercroft and guest hall. A sixteenth-century bridge across a huge moat leads to an impressive fifteenth-century gatehouse and a weatherboarded barn.

Warwickshire

MAXSTOKE PRIORY
Augustinian
10 miles east of Birmingham, 3 miles north of A45, by minor road north of Meriden. Ruins privately owned, but they can be seen from the churchyard.

This was one of the last Augustinian foundations, in 1336, but little survives other than two gatehouses, the west wall of the infirmary and part of the church

Maxstoke Priory, Warwickshire: one of the gatehouses.

Edington Priory, Wiltshire: the priory church.

crossing-tower. The gatehouse by the road allows a glimpse through to the inner gatehouse, converted to a house after the Dissolution, and now with farm buildings around.

MEREVALE ABBEY   Cistercian
1 mile west of Atherstone, ¹/2 mile south of A5, by B4116. Chapel by the gate in parochial use.

The abbey was founded in 1148, but little remains apart from the unusually large and rare example of a Cistercian *capella ante portas*, lopsided in plan, with a wide short nave, two-bay aisles and a four-bay chancel added in 1500 to the thirteenth-century church. There is a good Jesse window. Of monastic fragments east of the church, two walls of the frater stand to a good height, incorporated into farm buildings.

Wiltshire

EDINGTON PRIORY   Bonshommes
3¹/2 miles north-east of Westbury, in Edington village, off B3098. Church in parochial use.

Of this order, peculiar to Britain, only two houses were founded, at Ashridge, Hertfordshire, now replaced by a nineteenth-century mansion, and Edington, where the church is complete. Founded in 1351 as a secular college, it was converted in 1358 to a monastery whose occupants followed the Augustinian rule. Cruciform, with a central tower and freely embattled skyline, it was built between 1352 and 1361 by William of Edington, Bishop of Winchester. The three-bay chancel was the monastic quire, the nave for parishioners. The whole has delightful details both outside and inside, with charming plaster roofs of the seventeenth and eighteenth centuries, and some surviving medieval sculptures. No claustral buildings survive.

LACOCK ABBEY   Augustinian nuns
In Lacock village, 3 miles south of Chippenham, just east of A350. National Trust. House open April to October, daily, except Tuesdays, 1–5.30. Cloisters and grounds open March to October, 11–5.30.

Founded in 1232 by Ela, Countess of Salisbury, Lacock became an abbey in

1241, when she was the first abbess. It became a centre of education and aid for bereaved or sick women. In 1476 Lacock Abbey had two thousand sheep on its estates and owned a coal mine!

At the Dissolution Sir William Sharington bought the property and pulled down the church, using its stone for a courtyard adjoining his house, which was built around the cloisters and altered in the eighteenth and early nineteenth centuries. Three sides of the nuns' fifteenth-century cloister survive, remarkably little changed. Doors lead to a series of vaulted rooms: chaplain's room, sacristy, chapter-house, warming-room in the east range, with the refectory in the north range now divided into smaller rooms. The aisleless church was demolished; its north wall became the south wall of the Tudor mansion, with oriel windows inserted in 1830.

MALMESBURY ABBEY   Benedictine
In the centre of Malmesbury, 10 miles north of Chippenham, on A429. Church in parochial use.

Founded in 676 by St Aldhelm, Malmesbury Abbey became famous for its learning, prospered under King Athelstan's patronage, was pillaged by the Danes and damaged by fire in the eleventh century. A new abbey church was begun in 1143, and six bays of its nave, with a magnificent south porch, are in use today. Transepts, chancel and crossing-tower have gone, the latter collapsing just before the Dissolution.

Part of the Norman west front still stands, and the present east wall rests on the fifteenth-century pulpitum which formerly screened off the monastic quire. Piers and a wall of the south transept are all that remains of the eastern end. Claustral buildings were to the north. The hotel to the west incorporates some thirteenth-century fragments of the monastic guest-house.

Worcestershire

BORDESLEY ABBEY   Cistercian
Half a mile north-east of Redditch, signposted off the east side of A441 (Birmingham Road). Borough of Redditch. Open, April to September, Monday to Thursday daily, Saturday and Sunday afternoons; March, October, November, Monday to Thursday daily and Sunday afternoon. Closed December to January.

Founded in 1138, Bordesley Abbey was surrendered at the Dissolution in 1538, when the house was completely dismantled. The site has been virtually undisturbed, and since 1969 major archaeological excavations, setting new standards for study, have helped to define relationships between structure, liturgy, decoration and burial practices in a church where seven distinct floor levels have been identified. These range from the mid twelfth century to the late fifteenth century. Wall foundations help to reveal the monastic plan and many spectacular objects are well displayed in a modern visitor centre which contains an interpretative exhibition on Bordesley Abbey. Monastic workshops and a watermill have also been excavated.

EVESHAM ABBEY   Benedictine
Near the middle of Evesham. Precinct now a public park.

Founded in 701, Evesham Abbey was wholly rebuilt from the mid twelfth century, when it became important. Wealth accrued from its vast estates; but all has vanished except the glorious bell-tower, a freestanding campanile 110 feet (34 metres) high, open-arched at the base, with panelled sides and rich sculpture. It was completed in 1539. Nearby are the entrance arch to the late thirteenth-century chapter-house, and the almonry, now a museum.

GREAT MALVERN PRIORY   Benedictine

In the centre of Great Malvern. Most of monastic church in parochial use.

The priory was founded in 1085. All the claustral buildings went at the Dissolution, except for a heavily restored gatehouse. However, the church was saved, except for its south transept, and was restored by Scott in 1860–1. Externally it is Perpendicular at its most ornate, 1420–60, and contains the most complete and outstanding fifteenth-century stained glass in England. The short, round-piered nave betrays Malvern's Norman origins.

HALESOWEN ABBEY   Premonstratensian

In Halesowen off the A456 Kidderminster road, 6 miles west of Birmingham. English Heritage. Limited opening times.

The view from the B4551 on the hill south of the A466 roundabout reveals why the canons chose this site. They were enterprising farmers and the ruins of their abbey are incorporated into the present Manor Farm. What remains dates from the period 1220–30, a few years after the foundation. The south aisle wall of the nave is now the north wall of a barn. The north wall of the presbytery and some of the south transept walls survive. Farm buildings occupy the cloister area, where there is part of the south wall of the frater, with its undercroft. The canons' infirmary is a barn.

LITTLE MALVERN PRIORY   Benedictine

4 miles south of Great Malvern, off A4104. Church in parochial use. Little Malvern Court open mid April to mid July, Wednesday and Thursday afternoons.

The priory was founded in 1171. The present church consists of the chancel and tower of the monastic church, together with ruins of the transepts. Nearby Little Malvern Court, privately owned, incorporates part of the west claustral range, with the frater or prior's hall as its great hall.

PERSHORE ABBEY   Benedictine

Near the centre of Pershore, west of Market Place. Part of the monastic church in parochial use.

Founded for secular canons in 689, Pershore Abbey was refounded for Benedictines in 972, when it was richly endowed with estates. Nothing survives of the Norman monastery, except part of the church. The chancel was rebuilt about 1230, revaulted towards the end of the century. At the Dissolution the nave and Lady Chapel were demolished, and the north transept collapsed, the crossing-tower being shored up in 1686. The church is now gloriously islanded in a wide sward of fine lawns.

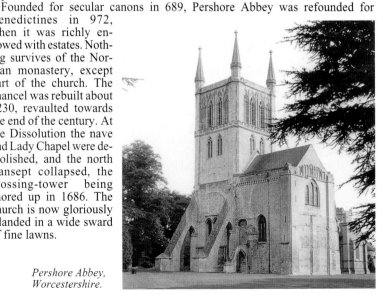

Pershore Abbey, Worcestershire.

WORCESTER CATHEDRAL-PRIORY — Benedictine
In the city, above the east bank of the river Severn. In episcopal use.

Founded in the late seventh century, Worcester was refounded in 961, and the present building was started in 1084. The exterior, ideally viewed from across the river, shows a smooth and thorough Victorian restoration. Inside are a superb early Norman crypt and twelfth-century transepts, with the remainder largely fourteenth-century, except for the fine chancel, which was started about 1220.

The cloisters to the south were rebuilt in the late fourteenth and early fifteenth centuries. The east walk has the usual slype, book recesses and circular Norman chapter-house, later recased and now decagonal. On the south side the frater, now part of the King's School, retains its undercroft, while the dorter, unusually, had an east-west axis from the west range. To the south-west are the substantial ruins of the infirmary. East of the cloister, the Edgar Gateway is a fourteenth-century structure, but with Victorian details.

Yorkshire

BOLTON PRIORY — Augustinian
5 miles north-west of Ilkley, by B6160. Nave used as parish church. Chancel and other ruins freely open.

Its riverside setting in the gracious landscape of lower Wharfedale has inspired many artists. The priory was founded at Embsay in 1120, but Bolton's canons moved here in 1154–5. The priory never became large or important and suffered from repeated Scottish raids.

Much of the early-fourteenth-century chancel and transepts stands to a good height, and earlier work survives in the nave, whose west front is masked by Prior Moon's west tower added in 1520. The Dissolution halted work, but the tower has been roofed and completed to serve as an entrance to the church. There are foundations of claustral buildings, and the gatehouse tower to the west was incorporated into a later mansion, Bolton Hall.

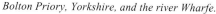

Bolton Priory, Yorkshire, and the river Wharfe.

BRIDLINGTON PRIORY   Augustinian
Church in parochial use.
Nothing remains *in situ* above ground of the priory founded in 1114. The
present church is the nave of a thirteenth-century building, together with the
north-west tower. The rest is mainly Sir George Gilbert Scott's restoration and
additions of 1876. The Bayle Gate is a late fourteenth-century gatehouse used
by priors as a courtroom.

BYLAND ABBEY   Cistercian
*By minor road 2 miles south of A170 between Thirsk and Helmsley. English
Heritage. Open daily April to October.*
Byland Abbey was founded on this site in 1177 after moving from near
Rievaulx. Extensive ruins are dominated by a memorable west front of the
church, including the lower half of a great rose window above Romanesque and
Gothic arches of 1200–25, when flamboyance had superseded earlier Cistercian
austerity. All the arcades and much of the nave south wall have been destroyed,
as have the claustral buildings, although the ground plan can be identified. This
shows the 'lane' separating the lay brothers' range from the west range of the
cloister. In the church large areas of yellow and green floor tiles survive, while
to the west one arch of a gatehouse spans the lane to Oldstead.

COVERHAM ABBEY   Premonstratensian
*2 miles south-west of Middleham. Ruins of the church visible from a public
bridleway; some of the guest-house incorporated into a later house, private.*
Founded in 1202 in Coverdale and damaged in fourteenth-century Scottish
raids, the abbey was rebuilt afterwards. Of the church, two bays of the nave
south arcade are prominent, with the west wall of the north transept. Remains of
the guest-house are incorporated into a late Georgian mansion and retain a fine
nine-light mullioned window of the late fifteenth or early sixteenth century,
with sculpture and an inscription. There is more sculpture about the mansion,
and the ruins of a single-arch gatehouse survive.

EASBY ABBEY   Premonstratensian
*1 mile south-east of Richmond, off B6271. English Heritage. Open freely
throughout the year.*
Founded in 1155 by the river Swale, the abbey is now approached through an
impressive gatehouse of 1300. Unusually, the parish church was built within
the precinct, between the gatehouse and the abbey, its vicar always being a
canon of the abbey.
Most of the abbey church has gone. South of it lay the cloister, with dorter,
reredorter and guest-house, unusually all on the west. The infirmary and
abbot's house were to the north, but the south range is the most impressive,
where the frater stands almost to full height, with a row of large windows above
a vaulted undercroft, all of about 1300.

FOUNTAINS ABBEY   Cistercian
*4 miles west of Ripon off B6265. National Trust and English Heritage. Open
daily throughout the year, except Fridays in November, December and January; also closed on 24th and 25th December.*
Fountains Abbey was founded in 1132 by reforming monks from the Benedictine St Mary's Abbey, York, who sought greater austerity in a wilder
environment. Wilderness was tamed in the wooded valley of the river Skell.
The monks acquired vast estates nearby and on the luscious limestone pastures
of the Pennines, where thousands of acres became vast sheep-walks, operated
from granges. Fountains became the wealthiest Cistercian monastery in Britain,

Fountains Abbey, Yorkshire, is now part of a World Heritage Site.

and the extensive abbey ruins reflect this.

Norman nave pillars of the vast church give way to the exquisite delicacy of the early thirteenth-century Chapel of the Nine Altars. Abbot Darnton's great west window typifies later changes in 1494. Abbot Huby's tower beyond the north transept added a spectacular finale to monastic building a few years later.

Claustral remains are so extensive that only the major survivals can be mentioned. These include the east, south and west ranges, with chapter-house, monks' frater, day stairs to the monks' dormitory, warming-house and kitchen. The great west range, with its cellarium beneath the lay brothers' dormitory, is unique. Arches of the lay brothers' reredorter show how the river Skell was skilfully used. Monastic guest-houses retain substantial masonry and window openings, and the abbey mill has been excavated. Fountains Abbey, together with the adjoining Studley Royal park and gardens, has been designated a World Heritage Site.

GUISBOROUGH PRIORY   Augustinian
In Guisborough town. Open daily all year.

Robert de Brus founded Guisborough Priory in 1129. In 1289 fire destroyed its church, which was rebuilt soon afterwards. This, coupled with devastating Scottish raids, drained the priory's financial resources. The church's east gable, nearly 100 feet (30 metres) high, dominates the meagre ruins, gauntly beautiful in statuesque decay, with a huge central window.

JERVAULX ABBEY   Cistercian
5 miles south-east of Leyburn, by A6108. Privately owned, but open daily throughout the year. Payment at an honesty box.

Founded at Fors, near Askrigg, in 1145, the abbey was moved to Jervaulx in 1156. Meagre ruins set in exquisite parkland are well looked after but avoid manicured perfection. Wild flowers add their own delights. The west wall of the monks' dorter is the outstanding survival, of 1200, and shows nine good lancets in its upper storey. To the east, high walls of the monks' infirmary survive.

KIRKHAM PRIORY   Augustinian
5 miles south-west of Malton on minor road off A64. English Heritage. Open daily April to October.
Founded in 1122, beautifully situated in the Derwent valley, Kirkham almost became Cistercian under the influence of one of its early priors, who subsequently joined the community at Rievaulx. Excavations have proved the existence of three churches, dating from 1130–40, 1160–70 and about 1230, when money ran out and the third, ambitiously planned, was never finished.
Foundations of many buildings reveal the monastic layout. In the west wall of the cloister are two fine arcades of the twin-bayed lavatorium, with only their lead-lined water troughs missing. Nearby is a reused Norman doorway. The gatehouse, 1320, is outstanding, richly sculptured on its outer, northern façade above a handsome rib-vaulted archway.

KIRKSTALL ABBEY   Cistercian
3 miles north-west of Leeds city centre, by A65. Leeds City Council. Free access to exterior of church and all monastic buildings.
Kirkstall Abbey was founded in 1147, from Fountains, and even more remains standing here, in urban parkland, than at the mother house in its tranquil rural setting. Church and monastic buildings were erected in the second half of the twelfth century and remain largely unaltered, apart from the crossing-tower added in the early sixteenth century, of which the gaunt south wall survives to full height, the east wall to about half its height. Views through arches and doorways reveal Norman and Transitional details, their masonry darkened through two centuries of industrial pollution.
Monastic quarters follow the usual Cistercian plan, with the east claustral range well-preserved, with library, chapter-house, parlour and day stairs to the dorter. There are foundations only of the infirmary, but substantial remains of the three-storey, thirteenth-century abbot's house. Much of the frater and adjacent kitchen survives, while the lay brothers' reredorter, extending to the west of their range, stands complete with roof and is used as a café.

MALTON PRIORY   Gilbertine
1 mile north-east of Malton, by A169. Part of the church in parochial use.
This is the rare survival of part of a church of Gilbertine canons, though missing its two eastern bays, clerestory and aisles. One western tower survives in the elegant west front of 1200, with a later five-light window.

MONK BRETTON PRIORY   Cluniac
2 miles east of Barnsley, off A633. English Heritage. Open throughout the year.
Founded about 1154, Monk Bretton became an independent Benedictine house in 1281. Barnsley's nearness is too apparent, but on a well-maintained site the church and east cloister range show little more than foundations and lower courses. The south wall of the frater and much of the west range are more impressive, with the prior's lodging showing a perfect two-light window near a handsome fireplace. There are inner and outer gatehouses and a restored structure which may have been a courthouse.

MOUNT GRACE PRIORY   Carthusian
7 miles north-east of Northallerton, off A19. English Heritage and National Trust. Open daily; except Mondays and Tuesdays, November to March.
Founded in 1398, this best-preserved of English charterhouses illustrates clearly how their monastic arrangements differed from those of other orders.

Monk Bretton Priory, Yorkshire.

Beautifully situated beneath a wooded hillside, its precinct enclosed two courts, roughly equal in size, with the small church and other communal buildings between forming the south side of the great cloister.

Around this irregular quadrangle were the fifteen individual cells of the monks, built in 1420–30. The interior of cell number 8 has been reconstructed, with interior walls repainted with limewash and windows glazed with new glass closely matching the medieval glass discovered in excavations. Furniture has been constructed, based on medieval prototypes, and the garden around the cell excavated and accurately replanted.

The monastic guest-house, ruined at the Dissolution, was incorporated into two later houses, a manor house of the Commonwealth period, and a larger house in 1900–1, in characteristic Arts and Crafts style. Restored and refurbished, this now houses a permanent exhibition illustrating the story of the Carthusians and the history of the house after the monks had gone.

NUN MONKTON Benedictine nunnery
7 miles north-west of York, by minor road off A59. Part of church in parochial use.

The western part of the aisleless nave now serves as the parish church. The graceful west façade shows two building periods: the lower part of 1170; the upper section, with its tall lancets, about sixty years later, presumably when the poor community could afford it. No domestic buildings survive.

RIEVAULX ABBEY Cistercian
2½ miles west of Helmsley on minor road off B1257. English Heritage. Open daily throughout the year.

Founded in 1131, Rievaulx was the first major British monastery of the reforming Cistercian order. Extensive, well-preserved ruins in the deeply wooded valley of the river Rye allow all main parts of a complex monastery to be understood. Under its third abbot, Ailred, 1147–67, Rievaulx thrived, and most of the claustral buildings were erected in his time, when there were probably

Roche Abbey, Yorkshire, stands in the centre of a 'Capability' Brown landscape.

140 choir monks and 600 lay brothers. The east range has substantial remains, but in the south range are arcaded canopies of the lavatorium and high walls of the early-thirteenth-century monks' frater and its undercroft.

Pillar bases in the church indicate its size – the earliest large Cistercian nave in Britain, used by the lay brothers. Beyond the transepts is Rievaulx's exquisite presbytery, added around 1225. Three-tiered walls of pale stone soar upwards, on arcades of pointed arches, breathtakingly beautiful, evidence not only of the monks' buildings skills but also of the softening of earlier Cistercian architecture.

A well-appointed visitor centre has displays illustrating the history of Rievaulx and the lives of its monks.

ROCHE ABBEY — Cistercian

1¹/₂ miles south of Maltby, off A634. English Heritage. Open daily, April to October.

Founded in 1147, Roche Abbey is beautifully situated in a valley beneath cliffs of white limestone. The walls of the east end of the church and transepts stand to a substantial height, the pointed arches of arcades and triforium suggesting a date around 1170, yet the clerestory has round-headed windows. Claustral wall footings reveal an almost perfect late twelfth-century Cistercian layout, with good use made of two streams for water supply and drainage.

SELBY ABBEY — Benedictine

In the centre of Selby. Church in parochial use.

The abbey was founded probably in 1069. The present abbey church, begun about 1100, survived intact both the Dissolution and later depredations, but all other monastic buildings have vanished. Restorations of 1871–3 and much rebuilding after a fire in 1906 do not detract from Norman splendour and Early English grace. Architectural historians will enjoy many happy hours identifying five different building phases in the nave alone.

Whitby Abbey, Yorkshire: the east end was built c.1220.

SWINE PRIORY   Cistercian
5 miles north-east of Hull, off A166. Church in parochial use.

The parish church is the late-twelfth-century chancel of the modest church of a nunnery founded in 1150. Unusually, the nuns used nave and transepts, demolished at the Dissolution. There are jolly little misericords on the choir-stalls.

WATTON PRIORY   Gilbertine
8 miles north of Beverley, off A164. Privately owned, but easily seen from the churchyard.

Founded in 1150 as a double house for nuns and resident canons, Watton Priory was probably the largest of the Gilbertine order. Only the prior's house survives, its fifteenth-century hall, with two-storeyed, five-sided window, forming the western range of the present house.

WHITBY ABBEY   Benedictine
On the clifftop, east of Whitby town centre. English Heritage. Open daily throughout the year. Visitor Centre.

Excavations have proved the existence of pre-Conquest buildings on the north side of the Norman and present abbey church, presumably of St Hilda's double monastery founded in 657. Whitby was refounded as a Benedictine priory in 1078, and it became an abbey early the following century. The church was rebuilt in the first half of the thirteenth century, its ruins now forming a spectacular sight on the cliffs. The north wall of the north transept survives to its full height, with three tiers of lancets topped by a rose window. The northern and eastern walls of the chancel are equally proud, with splendid arcading. The western part of the nave shows the change from lancet windows to wide ones with geometric tracery. Little remains of any other monastic buildings; the church alone in its windswept setting makes Whitby unforgettable.

YORK: ST MARY'S ABBEY   Benedictine
Just to the north of the city walls, on the north bank of the river Ouse, in Museum Gardens. Freely open, daily.

The abbey was founded in 1080 but only fragments of the church survive: part of the north wall of the north aisle, part of the west wall, and a pier arch of the crossing-tower. Wall footings and foundations reveal outlines of monastic buildings. Most is of the thirteenth and fourteenth centuries, as is much of the extensive precinct wall on the north and east, with the Great Gatehouse in Marygate, and other towers and posterns.

Principal monastic sites in Scotland

✢ ✢ ✢ ✢ ✢ ✢

Aberdeenshire

DEER ABBEY Cistercian
Near Old Deer, 10 miles west of Peterhead, on A950. Historic Scotland. Freely open at all reasonable times.

Deer Abbey was founded in 1219. Almost nothing survives of the church, but parts of the conventual buildings stand to a reasonable height. In the eastern range, the chapter-house, slype and parlour are identifiable, with rather more of the frater in the southern range, parallel to the cloister walk. A walled precinct encloses the riverside site.

Angus

ARBROATH ABBEY Tironensian
In Arbroath. Historic Scotland. Open daily, April to September; October to March, Monday to Saturday and Sunday afternoons.

The abbey was founded in 1176. There are very impressive remains of the late-twelfth- and early-thirteenth-century church, which had an aisled, nine-bay nave, north and south transepts each with two eastern chapels, a square-ended chancel, and twin western towers. The tall south transept, with rose window, is architecturally outstanding, but the west front, with recessed doorway, gablets and the lower half of an enormous round window, is rather marred by the later addition of a gatehouse range. Claustral buildings are ruinous, but the abbot's house to the west of the south range survives, dating from 1500 on an older undercroft, and is now a museum.

RESTENNETH PRIORY Augustinian
1¹/₂ miles east of Forfar. Historic Scotland. Freely open at all reasonable times.

Restenneth Priory was founded in 1153 but little remains except the tall square church tower, capped unusually by a shapely broach spire. There are

Arbroath Abbey, Angus: the west front.

Romanesque doorways at the foot of the tower, a fine thirteenth-century chancel and some medieval tombs. The nave and claustral buildings have gone, leaving only the silence of the centuries.

Argyll and Bute

ARDCHATTAN PRIORY   Valliscaulian
7 miles north-east of Oban, on the north side of Loch Etive, by minor road off A828. Historic Scotland (ruins only). Freely open at all reasonable times.

A Victorian house occupies much of the site of this priory founded in 1230. Until 1722, when a new kirk was built, the monastic choir was used parochially. The old church ruins contain early crosses and many seventeenth- and eighteenth-century monuments. The house, which is not open, incorporates the monastic frater.

Ayrshire

CROSSRAGUEL ABBEY   Cluniac
2 miles south-west of Maybole, on A77. Historic Scotland. Open daily April to September.

Founded in 1244, Crossraguel is one of only three Cluniac houses in Scotland. The thirteenth-century buildings were largely destroyed in the Scottish wars, and the extensive remains are mainly of the fourteenth and fifteenth centuries. The long narrow aisleless church, divided centrally by a gable-high screen wall, has walls to eaves height. Well-preserved claustral buildings of the east range include the sacristy and chapter-house, both vaulted, and the dorter undercroft with reredorter beyond, less well-preserved. Beyond is the unusual south court, where there were five small houses for corridiars (individuals granted subsistence and a place to live in a monastery). There are substantial ruins of the cellars of the abbot's lodging, and nearby is the imposing castellated gatehouse added in the mid sixteenth century when Crossraguel was held by a series of commendators appointed from outside the community. In the south-west corner of the precinct is a neat circular dovecote.

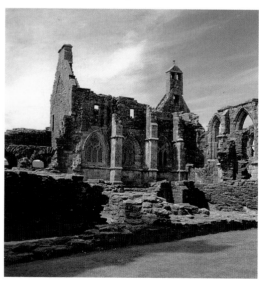

Crossraguel Abbey, Ayrshire: from the south-east, the extensive ruins from the fourteenth and fifteenth centuries.

Dumfries and Galloway

DUNDRENNAN ABBEY   Cistercian

6¹/₂ miles south-east of Kirkcudbright, off A711. Historic Scotland. Open daily April to September; October to March, Saturdays and Sunday afternoons.

Founded in 1142, Dundrennan was colonised by monks from Rievaulx, to which it bears a strong resemblance. Of the church little remains but the west end of the transepts, which have tall pointed arches, with blind arcading above and round-headed clerestory windows. In the cloisters to the south the western range is well preserved, with remains of a rectangular chapter-house, showing fine, thirteenth-century triple openings.

GLENLUCE ABBEY   Cistercian

8 miles east of Stranraer, 2 miles north-west of Glenluce village by minor road off A75. Historic Scotland. Open daily April to September; October to March, Saturdays and Sunday afternoons.

Founded in 1192, the seventh of twelve Cistercian abbeys in Scotland, its remains are fragmentary. Much of the church has gone but walls of the south transept and chancel stand to considerable height, with part of the monks' night stair. Of the claustral buildings to the south, the east range has the best survivals, with the chapter-house, rebuilt at the end of the fifteenth century, particularly well-preserved. Square, rib-vaulted in four bays, it has traceried windows, fine stone carving and medieval tiles. There are two barrel-vaulted rooms to its south.

LINCLUDEN COLLEGE   Benedictine

1 mile north of Dumfries, off A76, among the outer suburbs. Historic Scotland. Freely open at all reasonable times.

This was founded as a nunnery in 1164 but at the end of the fourteenth century it was repressed by the third Earl of Douglas, who established in its place a college of secular canons. The remains are those of the collegiate church and the sixteenth-century provost's house. Of the church, the chancel, south

Dundrennan Abbey, Dumfries and Galloway: the chapter-house.

aisle and transept survive, all of the early fifteenth century, together representing some of the best Decorated architecture remaining in Scotland, richly adorned with sculpture. The pulpitum, or stone screen separating chancel from nave, is particularly notable.

SWEETHEART ABBEY   Cistercian
In the village of New Abbey, 6 miles south of Dumfries, on A710. Historic Scotland. Open daily April to September; October to March, closed Thursday afternoons and Fridays.

Sweetheart Abbey was founded, in romantic circumstances, in 1273 by the Lady Devorgilla in memory of her husband, John Balliol, founder of Balliol College, Oxford, whose heart she kept in a casket which was later buried with her in the abbey in 1289. Only the late-thirteenth-century church survives, its red sandstone walls to eaves level, roofless but retaining a tall crossing-tower. The aisled nave has six bays, both transepts, each with two eastern chapels, and a two-bay, square-ended chancel. The west front stands to full height. Of monastic buildings little survives above foundation level, although after the Reformation the frater became the parish church until its demolition in 1731. An extensive amount of precinct wall, built of huge granite boulders, is an unusual survival.

WHITHORN PRIORY   Premonstratensian
At Whithorn on A750, 9 miles south of Wigtown. Historic Scotland. Open daily April to September; October to March, Saturdays and Sunday afternoons.

In an enclosed churchyard reached through an arch by the main street is a small roofless chapel, with the larger parish kirk of 1822 beyond. The ruin, with its aisleless nave and fine Norman doorways, was founded about 1175 and became the cathedral church of Galloway, served by Premonstratensian canons. The church was extended in the thirteenth century, with aisled transepts and chancel and a Lady Chapel. Only a crypt survives of these additions. Nearby is a museum containing a group of outstanding early Christian monuments and crosses, many predating the priory.

Edinburgh

HOLYROOD ABBEY   Augustinian
In Edinburgh, at the foot of the Canongate, in the grounds of the Palace of Holyroodhouse. Royal Palaces. Open April to October, Monday to Saturday and Sunday afternoons; November to March, daily, but shorter hours.

Founded by David I in 1128, the abbey was later absorbed into the seventeenth-century palace. The choir and transepts of the church went in 1569 and the claustral buildings were wholly demolished, but most of the early thirteenth-century nave survives. This had one of the earliest stone vaults in Scotland. A richly arcaded façade adds an air of unusual elegance, enhanced by the decoration on the west and south sides of the surviving north tower of the west front, with its unusual circular portrait medallions. The south tower was demolished to make way for the palace. When Charles I decided to be crowned at Holyrood, the west front was rebuilt on baroque lines but was subsequently mutilated. The five-light east window, inserted in 1633, was renewed in 1816.

Fife

CULROSS ABBEY   Cistercian
On the northern edge of Culross, 1 mile south of A985. National Trust for Scotland.

The abbey was founded in 1217 on a sloping site, with church above and claustral buildings down to the south. The nave of the church has gone, and the monastic quire became the parish church in 1633. The adjoining eighteenth-century manse incorporates some monastic survivals, and some undercrofts can be identified but are on private land.

DUNFERMLINE ABBEY   Benedictine
In Dunfermline. Part of the church in parochial use. Other monastic remains: Historic Scotland. Open daily April to September; October to March, closed Thursday afternoons and Fridays.

Founded as a priory about 1070 by Queen Margaret, second wife of King Malcolm Canmore, it became an abbey under David I. The twelfth-century nave, with its undertones of Durham, is probably the finest Norman church interior in Scotland. The site of the choir, rebuilt in the nineteenth century, is now the parish church, the thirteenth-century choir and transepts having been demolished at that time.

The cloister to the south is largely ruinous, although the frater walls stand almost to the eaves. The reredorter and its drain can be seen, while the guest-house across the road was converted into a royal palace, where Charles I was born.

INCHCOLM ABBEY   Augustinian
On Inchcolm in the Firth of Forth. Reached by ferry from South Queensferry (summer only) or from Aberdour. Historic Scotland. Open daily April to September.

Founded in 1123 as a priory, Inchcolm was raised to abbey status in 1235. Building continued, with several plan changes, up to the fifteenth century, but the final church is largely a ruin. Claustral ranges survive more completely here than anywhere else in Scotland and are unusual in having floors above the cloister walks. Fourteenth-century vaulted rooms include dorter, frater and guest hall, all roofed, on three sides, while the rare octagonal chapter-house has the warming-house above, with pyramidal roof and a fireplace, and reached by steps from the dorter. A large reredorter extended over the shore, so tides regularly flushed its drain.

ST ANDREWS CATHEDRAL AND PRIORY   Augustinian
In St Andrews. Historic Scotland. Open daily, April to September; October to March, Monday to Saturday and Sunday afternoons.

The site of a bishopric since 908, the priory was founded in 1133, with St

St Andrews Cathedral and Priory, Fife: the pinnacles of the eastern gable.

Rule's church probably the original priory church. Of the metropolitan cathedral, once Scotland's largest church, little survives except the tall, twin-pinnacled eastern gable, one pinnacle of the west gable, the wall of the south aisle of the nave, part of the south transept and a few pillars. Most claustral buildings have gone except for fragments of the east range, including the three-arched entry to the chapter-house. Ruins are mainly of the late twelfth and thirteenth centuries. Rows of gravestones add to the site's sadness.

Highland

BEAULY PRIORY   Valliscaulian
In Beauly, on A862. Historic Scotland. Freely open at all reasonable times.
    Three houses of this rare offshoot of the austere Cluniacs were founded in Scotland, this one in 1230. Only the small church survives, roofless, aisleless and cruciform, similar to the earliest Cistercian churches. Fourteenth- and sixteenth-century reconstruction includes a north chapel added to the nave.

Renfrewshire

PAISLEY ABBEY   Cluniac
In Paisley. Church of Scotland. Open daily.
    Founded by Walter Fitzalan in 1163, but destroyed by Edward I, the abbey was rebuilt and the present church dates mainly from the fifteenth century, with a fine west front and the St Mirin Chapel. Members of the Royal House of Stewart were buried here.

Scottish Borders

DRYBURGH ABBEY   Premonstratensian
3 miles south-east of Melrose, near St Boswells. Historic Scotland. Open daily, Monday to Saturday and Sunday afternoons.
    Founded in 1150 as Scotland's first Premonstratensian house, Dryburgh Abbey is beautifully situated in wooded surroundings by the river Tweed. The extensive ruins are on three levels. On the highest ground only the Early English transepts of the church survive. Considerable claustral remains, at a

Dryburgh Abbey, Scottish Borders: the north transept where Sir Walter Scott and Douglas Haig are buried.

Jedburgh Abbey, Scottish Borders, showing the nine bays of the nave of the church.

lower level, are reached through a twelfth-century processional doorway. The east range is well preserved, with sacristy, parlour, chapterhouse, day stairs to the dorter and steps leading down to the warming-house. The tall west gable of the frater still stands and has a fine wheel window. Most other buildings have gone apart from the ruins of a late-fifteenth-century gatehouse.

Beneath the vault of the north transept are the tombs of Sir Walter Scott, his son-in-law John Lockhart, Douglas Haig and his wife Dorothy.

JEDBURGH ABBEY   Augustinian

In Jedburgh, just off A68. Historic Scotland. Open daily, Monday to Saturday and Sunday afternoons.

The abbey was founded in 1138 by King David I of Scots. The ruins are dominated by those of the well-preserved church. Though roofless, its walls stand to full height from the west gable to the crossing-tower, with an aisled nave of nine bays, north and south transepts with apsidal chapels, a partially aisled chancel and a square-ended presbytery. Although the eastern end is more ruinous, the Norman arcades of the quire show an unusually interesting elevation. The superb west front of the church, with projecting porch, ornamented arches and blank arcading, is one of the finest Transitional pieces in Scotland. The central tower was rebuilt in the early sixteenth century.

Excavations have revealed much of the cloister layout; a visitor centre displays details and illustrations of the abbey's history.

Kelso Abbey, Scottish Borders: the late Norman work.

KELSO ABBEY   Tironensian
In Kelso. Historic Scotland. Freely open at all reasonable times.
Kelso Abbey was founded in 1128 by King David I, but only fragments of the church survive. These show a plan unique in Scotland, with western and eastern transepts, and towers over both crossings, as at Ely. The best-preserved part is the north transept and crossing, with part of a tower, in late Norman or Transitional style, all richly arcaded and with tiers of round-headed windows. There is nothing else except for a few cloister arches reconstructed to form a burial ground for the Dukes of Roxburgh.

MELROSE ABBEY   Cistercian
In Melrose. Historic Scotland. Open daily, Monday to Saturday and Sunday afternoons.
Founded by King David I in 1136–7, Melrose Abbey was colonised by monks from Rievaulx. The king's generous endowment ensured it was one of the wealthiest of Scottish abbeys, but the monastery was repeatedly damaged during the Scottish wars, worst of all in 1385 when the army of Richard II burned the church to the ground. The new church, built soon afterwards, was damaged in 1545, together with many of the monastic buildings.

The spectacular church ruins seen today are mainly of the early fifteenth-century rebuilding, when the Scottish Decorated architectural style was moving into the Perpendicular. There is an aisled nave of nine bays with a narrow north aisle, a wider south aisle having an adjoining extra aisle with eight chapels in it, north and south transepts each with two chapels, and a square-ended chancel with two chapels. The low ruins marking the west end of the nave date from the twelfth century.

Vaulting in the south transept and sanctuary survives, supported by flying buttresses, rare in Scotland. Masonry and sculpture in the south transept are superb, with carving both flamboyant and delicate.

Foundations only of the claustral buildings north of the church reveal the huge scale of this most impressive of Scottish monasteries.

Stirling

CAMBUSKENNETH ABBEY   Augustinian
1 mile east of Stirling, south of A91, reached across a field. Historic Scotland. Freely open at all reasonable times.
The abbey was founded in 1147 by King David I. Only the foundations of the church and claustral buildings can be seen, but the detached tower on the north side of the nave survives complete, a rare campanile built in the late thirteenth or early fourteenth century, with a vaulted ground floor and projecting stair turret.

INCHMAHOME PRIORY   Augustinian
On an island in the Lake of Menteith, reached by ferry from Port of Menteith, 4 miles east of Aberfoyle, off A81. Historic Scotland. Open April to September.
The priory was founded in 1238. In the church two bays of the nave's north arcade still stand, with the walls of the choir, but the tower is a later addition. Of the east claustral range, the barrel-vaulted chapter-house is well preserved, but little remains of the other ranges.

Principal monastic sites in Wales

✣ ✣ ✣ ✣ ✣ ✣

Carmarthenshire

TALLEY ABBEY   Premonstratensian
7 miles north of Llandeilo, off B4302. Cadw. Open daily.
   Founded for 'white' canons in 1184–9, this is the only Welsh monastery of the
Premonstratensian order. It has a beautiful situation, but little survives except the
central crossing and remains of the tower of the abbey church, a modest building
compared with what had been an architecturally ambitious plan.

Ceredigion

ST DOGMAELS ABBEY   Tironensian
1 mile west of Cardigan, by B4546. Cadw. Freely open.
   Founded in 1113–15, St Dogmaels Abbey suffered during the thirteenth-
century Edwardian wars and never prospered. Most buildings were heavily
ruined but their outlines can be seen, some walls standing to good heights. The
nave of the church was converted into the parish church after the Dissolution
and has much sixteenth-century masonry.

STRATA FLORIDA ABBEY   Cistercian
7 miles north of Tregaron by minor road off B4143. Cadw. Open daily.
   Founded in 1164 on a poor site, the abbey moved to the present one in 1184,
but church and monastic buildings were not completed until ninety years later.
Disasters followed: a severe fire, then much destruction during the Welsh
rebellion against Edward I. Next century Glendower's military occupation

Talley Abbey, Carmarthenshire.

Valle Crucis Abbey, Denbighshire.

caused further damage.

Strata Florida became an important centre for Welsh literature and culture: the National Annals of Wales were written there. Ruins on the south bank of the river Teifi consist mainly of low walls of the church, cloister and chapter-house. The early-thirteenth-century west doorway of the church is exquisite, framing a view of green hills beyond. The transept chapels are reroofed to protect medieval tiles reset in the floors. In their beautiful remote setting the ruins retain a tranquil atmosphere.

Denbighshire

VALLE CRUCIS ABBEY   Cistercian

1½ miles north-west of Llangollen, on A542. Cadw. Open daily.

Valle Crucis was founded in 1201 in a serene and tranquil valley. Good remains of the church retain high eastern and western walls and the well-preserved south transept with its high doorway from the monks' dormitory.

A disastrous fire necessitated much rebuilding from the mid thirteenth century. From the early fifteenth century the eastern range of the cloister survives, with its lovely, stone-vaulted chapter-house, the monks' dormitory above reached from the cloister by a stone stairway. The northern half of this was converted later in the century into a new hall for the abbot, with private chamber and fireplace, illustrating a drastic relaxation in the Cistercian way of life, with the abbot living in great comfort at the heart of the monastery. The monks' fishpond to the east gives a superb view of the abbey church and east cloister range.

Flintshire

BASINGWERK ABBEY   Cistercian
1 mile north-east of Holywell, off A548. Cadw. Always open.

Founded for Savignac monks in 1131, Basingwerk was later absorbed by the Cistercians and placed under the guardianship of Buildwas Abbey. Meagre ruins adjoin public playing fields, with parts of the chapter-house and monks' frater the best. The situation militates against any survival of sanctity.

Glamorgan

EWENNY PRIORY   Benedictine
1¹/₂ miles south of Bridgend by minor road off A48. Nave in parochial use.

The priory was founded in 1141 from St Peter's Abbey, Gloucester. The early twelfth-century nave, with massive Norman pillars, serves as a parish church. The roofed monastic choir and chancel and the south transept display fine Norman architectural detail in pale limestone, and the original stone altar table survives. The vault has unusually simple transverse ribs.

To the west and north, towers and two gatehouses and a high fortified perimeter wall give the precinct the character of a castle rather than a religious house. A stone stair gives access to a comfortable room above the vaulted arch of the southern gatehouse. A later mansion and its garden now occupy the site of the monastic cloister and domestic buildings.

MARGAM ABBEY   Cistercian
4 miles south-east of Port Talbot, off A48. Owned by Neath Port Talbot County Borough Council. Open daily except Monday and Tuesday in winter.

Founded in 1147 for monks from Clairvaux, Margam became the richest

Neath Abbey, Glamorgan: a Savignac foundation taken over by Cistercians.

Welsh monastery, with vast estates based on sheep-rearing. Later i became a centre for culture, arts and literature, producing many charters and manuscripts, but suffered during various Welsh uprisings. After the Dissolution successive mansions occupied the site, which now forms part of a country part.

All claustral buildings have gone except part of the infirmary vaul and, to the north, the exquisite polygonal chapter-house, with a twelve-sided exterior, circular inside, beautifully proportioned, built about 1200 but now roofless.

Most of the nave of the monastic church is a rare survival, in use as the parish church. It has a late-twelfth-century west doorway and nave piers, but there is much restoration of 1818.

NEATH ABBEY   Cistercian
1 mile west of Neath, off A465. Cadw. Open at all times.
Originally Savignac, founded in 1130, Neath Abbey was absorbed into the Cistercian order in 1147. Little is left of the church, rebuilt on an ambitious scale in 1280–1330, but there are extensive remains of claustral buildings, especially the west range. At the south-east corner of the cloister an early-sixteenth-century abbot's house was incorporated into an impressive Tudor mansion after the Dissolution, above the dormitory undercroft and monks' latrine. Walls and windows survive, but the beautiful rib-vaulted undercroft is, regrettably, locked. The mansion was abandoned in the early eighteenth century, and the whole site subsequently smothered in industrial waste. Today the surroundings are not impressive.

Gwynedd

CYMER ABBEY   Cistercian
2 miles north-west of Dolgellau, off A494. Cadw. Open daily.
Cymer was founded in 1198 in a remote setting at the head of the Mawddach estuary. The Edwardian wars probably curtailed ambitious building plans. Ruins of the simple rectangular church retain good lancet windows at the east and the northern arcade of the nave. There are few remains of the claustral layout, but the adjoining farmhouse probably incorporates the remains of the monastic guest-house.

Monmouthshire

LLANTHONY PRIORY   Augustinian
In the beautiful Honddu valley, 9 miles north of Abergavenny by B4423. Cadw. Open freely.
The priory was founded in 1118 but the canons were forced to abandon the site after the Welsh national rising of 1135. They returned towards the end of the twelfth century and started rebuilding. Extensive remains of the church survive, all of 1180–1230, with the eight-bay aisled nave, two high walls of the crossing-tower and the well-preserved western towers, one being incorporated into the Abbey Hotel together with the west range of the cloister. The transept chapels were unusually long, and the eastern claustral range has remains of the chapter-house. To the south of the cloister, the thirteenth-century St Mary's church may have been the monastic infirmary. Nearby farm buildings conceal the priory gatehouse.

TINTERN ABBEY   Cistercian
4¹/₂ miles north of Chepstow, by A466. Cadw. Open daily throughout the year.
Founded in 1131, Tintern was only the second Cistercian house to be established in Britain. Its Wye valley setting makes it one of the most memorable

Tintern Abbey, Monmouthshire, is set attractively in the Wye valley.

of all Britain's ruined monasteries. Growing numbers of monks by the end of the twelfth century necessitated major rebuilding. The great church, now roofless but standing almost to the original height, dates largely from 1270–1300, by when all earlier Cistercian ideas of austerity had gone.

Claustral buildings are placed, unusually, to the north, probably because of the needs of water supply and drainage. Outlines are almost complete, and some walls stand to considerable height, particularly on the western and northern ranges, where the outer parlour, monks' frater, warming-house and novices' lodging are prominent. The north wall of the north transept shows the roof line of the monks' dormitory, with the night stairs within the transept. Details delight, such as recesses in a corner of the dining-hall where dishes were washed and stored, twelfth-century book cupboards in the east cloister walk, and remains of the collation seat in the south cloister walk.

Powys

BRECON CATHEDRAL-PRIORY   Benedictine
On the northern edge of the town. Since 1923 the priory church has been the cathedral for Swansea and Brecon diocese.

The church is mainly thirteenth- and fourteenth-century, with the four-bay chancel a beautifully pure example of Early English, stone-vaulted in 1861. Nave and aisles were developed later, with additional chapels representing the increased prosperity of Brecon from 1300. Although no early conventual buildings survive, there is an impressive fifteenth-century precinct wall with two gateways, a canonry tower of the early sixteenth century, a small almonry and an early-seventeenth-century tithe barn.

Other monastic sites

✢ ✢ ✢ ✢ ✢ ✢

Most of these have only scanty remains, often incorporated into farm buildings or private houses not normally accessible to the public, although they may be visible from the highway or public footpath.

The order that owned each monastery is given in brackets after the name. The following abbreviations are used: A, Augustinian; B, Benedictine; C, Cistercian; Cl, Cluniac; P, Premonstratensian.

England

BUCKINGHAMSHIRE
Chetwode (A): part of priory church in parochial use.
Medmenham (C): fragments have been incorporated into a later mansion.

CAMBRIDGESHIRE
Anglesey Abbey (A): some thirteenth-century fragments incorporated into a later mansion (NT).

CUMBRIA
Wetheral Priory (B): gatehouse and some precinct wall.

DERBYSHIRE
Repton (A): gatehouse and probable guest-house are now part of the buildings of Repton School.

DEVON
Canonsleigh (A): gatehouse within farm buildings.
Cornworthy (A): gatehouse.
Dunkeswell (C): gatehouse fragments. Early Victorian church contains medieval tiles and tombs.
Exeter: St Nicholas (B): guest-house with undercroft.
Plympton (A): fragments of walls in St Mary's churchyard.

DORSET
Bindon (C): low foundation walls. Part of Bindon House.
Tarrant Crawford (C): Abbey Farm on site. South side of present church may have adjoined monastic buildings.

ESSEX
Barking (B): gatehouse.
Beeleigh (P): east claustral range incorporated into a private house.
Latton (A): crossing of church incorporated into a barn.

GLOUCESTERSHIRE
Cirencester (A): site now a public park. Some precinct wall and a Norman gateway.
Gloucester: Llanthony (A): part of gatehouse and barn ruins.

HAMPSHIRE
Mottisfont (A): parts of church and claustral range incorporated into mansion (NT).
Winchester: Hyde Abbey (B): gatehouse.

HEREFORDSHIRE

Craswall (Grandmontine): low walls and overgrown fragments of masonry in remote valley below Black Mountains.

Flanesford (A): frater now part of private house.

Wigmore (A): inner gatehouse and fragments of other buildings, part of farm.

KENT

Bilsington (A): infirmary hall and undercroft incorporated into an Edwardian house.

Boxley (C): gatehouse and tithe barn. Other buildings incorporated into a private house.

Dover (A): gatehouse and guest-house now part of Dover College.

Lesnes (A): low walls and foundations in public park.

Monks Horton (Cl): part of church and west claustral range now part of private house.

LEICESTERSHIRE

Grace Dieu (A): crumbling walls, mainly of chapter-house.

LINCOLNSHIRE

Barlings (P): wall fragments of church and some carved masonry in nearby cottage.

Lincoln: St Mary Magdalen (B): parts of chancel.

Newstead (Gilbertine): site occupied by farm.

Stamford: St Leonard's (B): west front and north arcade of small, early Norman church.

Thornholme (A): parish church contains some fragments.

Tupholme (P): frater wall, with lancets and pulpit.

NORFOLK

Beeston (A): substantial walls of church, nave and chancel.

Broomholm (Cl): gatehouse, transept of church and fragments of other buildings.

Coxford (A): arch, and other fragments of church.

Hickling (A): fragments of claustral range among farm buildings.

Horsham St Faith (B): site occupied by farm.

Langley (P): farm buildings incorporate many fragments from claustral range.

Marham (C): nave wall in Abbey House garden.

Pentney (A): gatehouse.

St Benet of Hulme (B): gatehouse.

West Acre (A): gatehouse and barn.

NORTHUMBERLAND

Alnwick (P): gatehouse and monks' well.

Newminster (C): re-erected cloister arcades at Abbey Farmhouse. (Permission needed to visit.)

SOMERSET

Montacute (C): splendid gatehouse, with possible guest-house adjoining.

Stavordale (A): fifteenth-century priory church converted into private house after Dissolution.

SUFFOLK

Butleigh (A): magnificent gatehouse (private).

St Benet's Abbey gatehouse and mill are a well-known feature of the Norfolk Broads. The last abbot was appointed Bishop of Norwich in 1536 and St Benet's was not dissolved, the only religious house to survive. Bishops of Norwich remain abbots of St Benet's and the rector of Horning is also the prior. He leads an annual pilgrimage to the ruins on the first Sunday in August.

Herringfleet: St Olave's (A): nave, cloister garth, frater undercroft.
Sibton (C): frater walls. North wall of cloister.

SUSSEX
Easebourne (A): some claustral buildings incorporated into a later house. Frater restored for parish use.
Tortington (A): part of nave arcade now in farmyard.
Wilmington (B): gatehouse and remains of domestic buildings around parish church.

WARWICKSHIRE
Coombe near Coventry (C): chapter-house entrance and a few other fragments, in public park.
Coventry (B): wall fragments, pillars and arches of former cathedral-priory.
Kenilworth (A): gatehouse and guest-house and wall foundations of parts of church.
Stoneleigh (C): gatehouse and guest-house adjoining. Parts of church incorporated into eighteenth-century mansion.

WILTSHIRE
Bradenstoke (A): undercroft of west cloister range and part of church tower.

YORKSHIRE
Ellerton (C): church tower.
Lastingham (B): apsidal crypt of parish church, 1088, survives from monastic church. Rare and beautiful.

Richmond: St Martin's (B): many recognisable fragments, especially of church, by a farm.
Rosedale (C): buttressed turret. Masonry fragments in nearby houses.

Scotland

AYRSHIRE
Kilwinning (B): walls of church transepts, tower, part of nave, some doorways, in churchyard of parish kirk.

FIFE
Balmerino (C): vaulted chapter-house, sacristy and other scanty remains (NTS).

SCOTTISH BORDERS
Coldingham (B): choir of priory church, early-thirteenth-century, restored for parochial use.

Wales

CONWY
Aberconwy (C): west tower of abbey church, now part of parish church.

ISLE OF ANGLESEY
Penmon (A): part of priory church in parochial use. Priory dovecote.

MONMOUTHSHIRE
Abergavenny (B): priory church in parochial use.
Chepstow (B): nave of priory church in parochial use.

POWYS
Abbeycwmhir (C): a few pier bases, wall fragments and isolated bits of carved masonry, in a lovely valley. Five arcade bays re-erected at Llanidloes parish church.

Monasteries today

✣ ✣ ✣ ✣ ✣ ✣

Monasticism in Britain did not end with the Dissolution. Indeed, there are more than a dozen monasteries existing today, most of them of the Benedictine order. As in the days of the medieval monasteries, today's monks take their vows and give their lives to God, sometimes in seclusion from the world, and sometimes through work as well as prayer. Some twentieth-century monasteries are kept going by the sale of goods made, and most of them welcome visitors and pilgrims who are genuinely interested in their work.

Ampleforth, North Yorkshire, is a Benedictine community, together with a fine school, descended from the foundation at Westminster.

Aylesford Priory, Maidstone, Kent. The Friars, the traditional name of the priory, was founded by the Carmelites in 1242 and after the Dissolution became a private mansion. The Carmelites regained possession in 1949, and The Friars now blends medieval and new buildings. Its chapels contain many modern examples of religious art. Fine pottery is made, and the Community of Carmelite Friars, as a centre of prayer and pilgrimage, welcomes visitors.

Belmont, Herefordshire, has an early Victorian church for its Benedictines.

Buckfast Abbey, Devon, is a Benedictine monastery occupying since 1882 the site of a medieval monastery. The new church of the abbey, built by the monks themselves, was finished in 1938 after thirty-one years of work.

Caldey Island, off the Pembrokeshire coast, is reached by boat from Tenby. The Cistercian monks grow their own produce and sell some. The medieval priory buildings are still used.

Douai, near Reading, Berkshire, is Benedictine.

Downside Abbey, near Bath, has the biggest and stateliest monastic church of the twentieth century, started in late Victorian times. Buildings of the famous school adjoin. Benedictine.

Farnborough, Hampshire, is a Benedictine monastery, where monks design Christmas cards and rear silkworms.

Garvald, East Lothian. Cistercian monks re-established a monastic community in 1946 and have added many new buildings to an existing mansion and medieval tower on the Nunraw estate.

Iona, Argyll and Bute. Here there are ruins of the thirteenth-century priory church of an Augustinian nunnery. The nearby Benedictine abbey, elevated to cathedral status in the sixteenth century, was

Buckfast Abbey in Devon is a popular visitor attraction.

Mount St Bernard, Leicestershire: the architect A. W. N. Pugin worked on the design of the monastery.

restored between 1899 and 1912 for public worship. The monastic buildings were restored between 1938 and 1965 and are now the centre of the Iona Community, founded by Dr George MacLeod and dedicated to the work of the church throughout Scotland.

Mount St Bernard, near Loughborough, Leicestershire, is a Cistercian foundation in Charnwood Forest, where monks have their own farm and make pottery.

Pluscarden, Moray. The medieval monastic site was given to Benedictines from Prinknash, who since 1948 have carried out an extensive rebuilding programme. There is outstanding modern glass in the church.

Prinknash, near Gloucester, was established in 1928 by Benedictine monks in a Tudor manor house in the Cotswolds. Fine new monastic buildings were opened in 1972. The monastery is largely self-supporting from the estate produce and the sale of its famous pottery.

Quarr, Isle of Wight, is Benedictine, with a church designed by a monk.

Ramsgate, Kent, has a Benedictine monastery.

Further reading

✣ ✣ ✣ ✣ ✣ ✣

The official guidebooks to the various religious houses in the care of English Heritage, Historic Scotland or Cadw are recommended for their authoritative and clear accounts, together with excellent layout plans.

Abbeys: An Introduction to the Religious Houses of England and Wales. HMSO, 1978. The official general guide.

Aston, Michael. *Monasteries*. Batsford, 1993.

Baskerville, Geoffrey. *English Monks and the Suppression of the Monasteries.* Weidenfeld & Nicolson, 2002.

Butler, L., and Given-Wilson, C. *Medieval Monasteries of Great Britain.* Michael Joseph, 1978.

Coppack, Glyn. *Abbeys and Priories*. Batsford/English Heritage, 1990.

Coppack, Glyn. *Fountains Abbey*. Tempus, 2003.

Crossley, F. H. (revised by Bryan Little). *The English Abbey*. Batsford, 1962.

Fawcett, Richard. *Historic Scotland Book of Scottish Abbeys and Priories*. Batsford, 1994.

Knowles, David. *The Monastic Order in England*. Cambridge University Press, 1940.

Knowles, David. *The Religious Orders in England* (three volumes). Cambridge University Press, 1948, 1955 and 1959. The most authoritative and comprehensive treatment of the whole subject.

Knowles, David. *Bare Ruined Choirs: Dissolution of the English Monasteries.* Cambridge University Press, 1976.

Midner, Roy. *English Medieval Monasteries 1066–1540. A Summary.* Heinemann, 1979.

Platt, C. *The Abbeys and Priories of Medieval England.* Secker & Warburg, 1984.

Thorold, Henry. *Collins Guide to Ruined Abbeys of England, Wales and Scotland.* Harper-Collins, 1992.

William, David H. *The Welsh Cistercians* (two volumes). Caldey Island, Tenby, 1983–4.

The Ordnance Survey Map of Monastic Britain (two sheets) is extremely useful.

The garden at Buckland Abbey, Devon.

Index

✤ ✤ ✤ ✤ ✤ ✤

Page numbers in italic refer to illustrations.